St Michael's Coventry

The Rise and Fall of the Old Cathedral

RAMP

George Demidowicz and Heather Gilderdale Scott

Introduction by Jonathan Foyle

St Michael's Coventry

The Rise and Fall of the Old Cathedral

COVENTRY CATHEDRAL

WORLD MONUMENTS FUND BRITAIN

Generous support for this publication was provided by The Paul Mellon Estate

SCALA

First published in 2015 by
Coventry Cathedral
Youell House
1 Hill Top
Coventry CV1 5AB
www.coventrycathedral.org.uk

In association with
Scala Arts & Heritage Publishers Ltd
10 Lion Yard
Tremadoc Road
London SW4 7NQ, UK
www.scalapublishers.com

ISBN 978-1-85759-929-9

Edited by Jessica Hodge
Designed by James Alexander
at Jade Design
Printed in India

10 9 8 7 6 5 4 3 2 1

FRONTISPIECE: The surviving tracery of the east end windows framing the tower beyond; the canopy that links old St Michael's with the new cathedral can be seen at right

PHOTO CREDITS
Commissioned photography of St Michael's courtesy of Andy Marshall

Jonathan Foyle: pp. 10, 11
George Demidowicz: pp. 16, 21, 23 below, 24, 27, 28, 36 below, 46 top
Herbert Art Gallery & Museum, Coventry: pp. 25, 60, 62 below, 63 top, 70
Warwickshire County Record Office: pp. 35 top, 54, 61 top, 77 right
Birmingham Museum and Art Gallery: pp. 47 below
British Library: pp. 56, 109
Archives and Heritage, Birmingham Central Library: pp. 62 top, 64, 100 top
Coventry Archives and Local Studies (History Centre): pp. 63 below, 67 top, 68 both, 72 both, 76
Lambeth Palace Library, London: p.65
Society of Antiquaries Library, London: p.66
RIBA Library Drawings & Archives Collection: pp. 73 top, 78
Museum of Fine Arts, Boston: p.110 top

Foreword 6
The Very Reverend John Witcombe, Dean of Coventry Cathedral

Introduction 7
Jonathan Foyle, Former Chief Executive, World Monuments Fund Britain

St Michael's: The Building 12
George Demidowicz

1. The old cathedral 15
2. Origins and historical background 16
3. From castle chapel to parish church 24
4. From parish church to cathedral 51
5. From destruction to world monument 81

St Michael's: The Medieval Stained Glass 96
Heather Gilderdale Scott

1. The history of the glass 99
2. The iconography of the fifteenth-century glazing scheme 102
3. Glaziers at St Michael's 119

Acknowledgments 126
Bibliography 126
Index 127

Foreword

The Very Reverend John Witcombe, Dean of Coventry

St Michael's Cathedral today is open to the sky. Many visitors find that searing openness incredibly moving, a place of openness to the trauma of the world, but also to the reality of God's presence in the midst of destruction. Week by week the present-day cathedral community recite the 'Coventry Litany of Reconciliation' in front of the rough stone altar, the charred cross, and windowless apse. It is a prayer for forgiveness and hope for ourselves and our broken world, which unites a worldwide community of people working for Peace and Reconciliation, in the Community of the Cross of Nails.

The power of the iconic ruins of Coventry Cathedral springs from the grandeur that was destroyed in the days of the Blitz. This book opens the past to us, to help us understand the riches that were lost. In describing them to us, George Demidowicz helps us to grasp where we have come from – and in so doing helps today's readers to participate in the trajectory of new hope and life which was set in the construction of the new cathedral, so wonderfully incorporating the shell of the old building into one glorious journey from destruction to new life, from death to resurrection.

You will also find in the following pages an introduction to the extraordinary medieval glass which was removed from the building before its destruction, and which has now been catalogued and restored prior, we hope, to being displayed in a new glass installation in the new cathedral. Every day we are invited to be 'made new' by the Spirit of God: as you enjoy this book, may you know for yourselves the excitement and inspiration both of those who raised the first St Michael's Cathedral, and of those who continue the Coventry story today, transforming division and brokenness into peace and hope.

We are very grateful to those who have enabled us to bring this story to life and to safeguard its continuing power, both in the restoration of the ruins and the preservation of the medieval glass, and in the telling of the story that follows. In particular, I would like to thank Dr Jonathan Foyle and World Monuments Fund Britain, in close partnership with the Paul Mellon Endowment for Architectural Conservation in Great Britain, alongside generous support from the Dr Mortimer and Theresa Sackler Foundation, American Express, the Aldama Foundation and English Heritage, amongst many others. This project is just one example of the rediscovery and celebration of Coventry's rich historical and artistic heritage, which is being presented afresh both to residents and to visitors to the city through a lively collaboration of professional organisations, academics and funders, working together with the City Council and, in St Michael's, with the Dean and Chapter, to revitalise the cathedral quarter and make it a worthy destination for any visitor. This is part of an ongoing programme to encourage appreciation for Coventry Cathedral and refresh the way its environment and treasures are presented, which in turn will help the cathedral to better fulfil its essential mission, both locally and across the world.

Introduction

Jonathan Foyle, Former Chief Executive, World Monuments Fund Britain

The most common reaction to an introductory visit to the surviving medieval arts of Coventry is, 'who knew?' My response is usually, 'too few'. There are good reasons why Coventry's wonders are under-appreciated, hidden in plain sight in the heart of England. The A4053, better known as the ring road, certainly doesn't help. The view from it is a parade of underwhelming modern buildings, and their concrete reinforces many prejudices. Old Coventry may seem lost to any who have seen the grim black-and-white footage of its bombing on 14 November 1940, and the city is still remembered for another wave of devastation – the dissolution of its engineering industries in the 1980s. One might think of Coventry as a mass of cheap, recent building. But look more carefully. There in the heart of the city, three spires rise. They mark the cathedral quarter, one of the great medieval experiences of England.

What none of us remember is that, in the fourteenth century, Coventry was the fourth richest city in England. As George Demidowicz explains, the city was divided into two halves which met at the hilltop. The cathedral priory of St Mary and church of Holy Trinity presided over the northern half, while the southern was home to the merchants and mayors based in St Mary's Guildhall. The Guildhall occupied the site of Coventry Castle, which had been ruined in the twelfth century, and St Michael's church was once the castle chapel. The money Coventry's merchants made from its cloths, hats and other prestigious goods was poured into beautiful civic and religious buildings, defended by the city walls. The boomtime for building, carving, glazing and painting was the early fifteenth century; then, in the 1450s, the Wars of the Roses began.

It is this crucial era – between the reigns of Henry VI (1422–61; 1470–71) and Henry VII (1485–1509) – that Coventry's medieval culture illustrates better than anywhere else. Six hundred year-old arts, as ancient as the early masters of the Italian Renaissance, still eloquently portray Coventry's role as a power-base in the heartlands of the Lancastrian monarchy, a relationship that remained potent at the accession of the Tudors. The most startling survival is the interior north wall of St Mary's Guildhall. On that single plane, in a room that was used for parliament when Westminster became too volatile in the 1450s, a wonderful ensemble of arts reveals the self-image of two rulers of England and their relationship to a city known as the '*Camera Principis*', the Prince's Chamber, so favoured by Edward the Black Prince (1330–76), son of Edward III and the royal patron of Cheylesmore Manor. The stained glass window shows Henry VI at the centre of its nine lights. It was probably made in the 1450s. The king and his queen, Margaret of Anjou, came to Coventry several times in that decade, visiting St Michael's in 1451, when Henry VI made Coventry a county in its own right. The monarchs led pageants past the great church and along Bayley Lane, to the Guildhall. Here, Henry treated the mayor to a sermon on good governance.

When the 1455 battle of St Albans opened the conflict between the Lancastrian house of Henry VI and the rival Yorkist claimants to the throne, Coventry became an alternative seat of parliament in the midst of national turmoil. By now Henry VI

OVERLEAF: *The richly weathered façade of St Mary's Guildhall faces St Michael's across Bayley Lane*

had become mentally unstable, and perhaps for this reason it was Queen Margaret who led a pageant through the city on 14 September 1456, intended to emphasise their quasi-divine status. At the city gates, she met the characters of the holy monarch Edward the Confessor, and St John the Evangelist. Further biblical and historical personifications she encountered included her namesake St Margaret, defeating the tyrannical dragon, and a feigning Julius Caesar, who proclaimed:

> I, Julius Cesare, souerayn of knyghthode
> And emperowr of mortall men, most hegh & myghty,
> Welcum you, princes most benynge & gode;
> Of quenes that byn crowned so high non knowe I.
> *The Coventry Leet Book*

The king's incapacity may well have made such political imagery even more important, especially so for the city's 1459 *Parliamentum diaobolicum*, which imposed punitive measures on the defeated Duke of York and his supporters. The great window surely provided its backdrop. Henry VI is portrayed confidently in a row of notably militant or Christian regal ancestors, including Emperor Constantine, Richard the Lionheart, his namesakes Henry III, IV and V, William the Conqueror and even King Arthur. The comparison is clear: Henry VI is to be seen as a righteous warrior defending his realm. And tellingly, he is accompanied by Edward III, the king from whom the houses of York and Lancaster both claimed descent, and who had given Coventry the right of a mayor in 1345. If the king paid for the glass, it was an investment in the hearts and minds of wealthy Coventrians, who had so recently built St Michael's church and steeple as an ornament to his kingdom; if the mayor or merchants paid for it, the window reflected the king's preconceptions.

Around 40 years later, the Bruges tapestry was woven for the same wall – the fictive columns that divide it into three sections align with the main mullions of the window above. It may have been a gift from the 'nephew' of Henry VI, his namesake Henry VII (1485–1509), the first Tudor monarch, who first came to Coventry soon after his defeat of the Yorkist Richard III on 22 August 1485 at the battle of Bosworth, just 15 miles north-east of Coventry. He was presented with £100 and a cup. Henry and Queen Elizabeth of York visited the city again in 1500, and so perhaps they gave the tapestry in that year. It would have been in their interest to have made such a gift, as it shows Henry VI and Margaret of Anjou, who had so favoured Coventry in the 1450s, praying to the Assumption of the Virgin, which the late king had experienced as a vision three times, a sure sign of his saintliness. The piece was probably commissioned in the late 1490s, after Henry VII had launched a papal campaign to canonise Henry VI; a Lancastrian saint would augment his bloodline and reinforce his God-given authority to rule. And so in 1503 Henry VII's Chapel in Westminster was begun as a mausoleum to hold the hallowed remains. But this campaign failed; Henry VI's body stayed at Windsor, and Coventry was left with the rich artistic propaganda.

Somehow – amazingly – when Cromwell's troops visited Coventry in the 1640s and slighted its fifteenth-century walls, the stained glass kings survived, and the tapestry's image of God was carefully concealed by the present figure of Justice, much more acceptable to the Puritan age. From the evidence of just this one nationally-important wall, it is clear that Coventry is a city with an immense and ancient story to tell. Through half a millennium of wars, riots and repairs, the medieval city avoided the fires that ravaged many timber-built towns and there

The magnificent interior of the Guildhall, with a specially-commissioned Bruges tapestry echoing the design of the heraldic window above it, bears witness to Coventry's political and artistic significance in the fifteenth century

The Guildhall's window is a powerful exercise in political image-making, with Henry VI portrayed as the virtuous warrior-king, among a group of real and mythical predecessors that includes the Emperor Constantine, William the Conqueror and King Arthur

is much else to explore that fills out a thousand years of history.

But in any account of Coventry, the old cathedral church that this book discusses is focal: its exceptionally beautiful spire may well mark the centre of medieval England. World Monuments Fund was brought (rather than sent) to Coventry precisely because of the cathedral quarter's power to inform and inspire, and the potential it offered to make a better city by using it important historic assets more effectively. In 2012, the year that the crumbling ruins of old St Michael's were placed on the World Monuments Watch, the fact that 12,000 pieces of stained glass, constituting the nation's largest corpus of loose medieval fragments, lay in the basement of Sir Basil Spence's modern cathedral was virtually unknown. In 2012–13, Crick Smith Conservation (University of Lincoln) cleaned and repaired the glass, and Dr Heather Gilderdale Scott brilliantly analysed the significance of its vividly drawn characters and lively colours. Meanwhile, the shattered, grand building it came from was virtually raised from the ruins by George Demidowicz as he depicted, through careful, groundbreaking scholarship, one of the greatest churches of medieval Britain, substantial enough to become a cathedral.

Coventry is a city that should be better known. The World Monuments Watch provided a way of elevating this hidden story, and both the conservation work and support for this book are investments toward the future understanding and care of Coventry's past. Understanding starts by sharing as widely as possible this new knowledge of the long history of St Michael's and the grand scheme of glazing that it displayed. We hope that this eye-opening book can play a small part in helping the institutions that share the cathedral quarter to build the esteem and reputation it deserves, and thus generate support for its future. Until then, you can take advantage of enjoying its manifold wonders undisturbed.

St Michael's: The Building

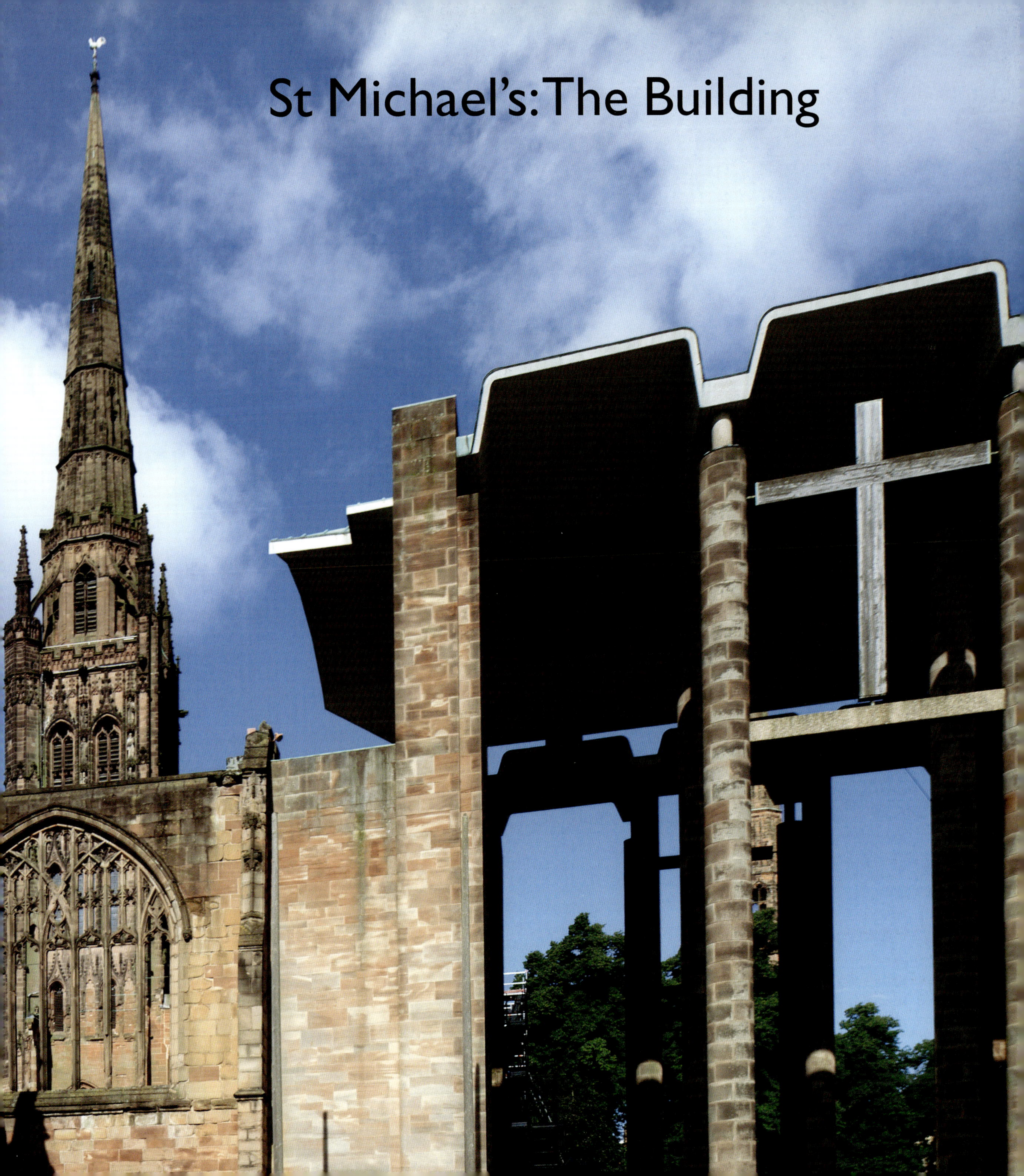

1. The old cathedral

It is ironic that only through its destruction in a German air raid on the night of 14 November 1940 did the cathedral of St Michael become known throughout the world. Before that date its fame was of a national order, as one of the largest parish churches in the country, elevated to cathedral status as late as 1918. Its architecture also attracted much wonder, with its magnificent tower and spire and the masterful application of the Perpendicular Gothic style.

The trauma caused by its devastation may explain why no single book has been devoted to the history of St Michael's. The memory of what was lost would have been painful and thoughts quickly turned to its replacement. This book is intended to remedy the situation, for the cathedral remains a building of national importance with a rich and fascinating history.

LEFT: *The spire of St Michael's was one of the tallest in medieval England; work on it began in the 1370s, soon after the construction of St Mary's Guildhall*
RIGHT: *Much of the decorative detailing on the tower dates from the Victorian restoration*

The focus in this section will be on the architecture and archaeology of the cathedral, chronicling its origins and development, then its gradual deterioration before major restoration in the late nineteenth century. The new and expensively repaired fabric was destined to last for just half a century and may have accelerated the collapse of the roofs once the incendiaries caught hold during the November air raid.

The cathedral is an embodiment of human belief and endeavour. Its fabric reflects both the spiritual and the material aspirations of the people, some whose names are known, others anonymous, who erected and beautified it. Their handiwork and investment is still there to be seen. Had not Coventry become one of the most prosperous towns in medieval England, its parish church would never have attracted the numerous chantry chapels and altars that were intended to guarantee a place in heaven for the wealthiest of Coventrians.

This section is based on the author's conservation plan, commissioned by the World Monuments Fund Britain and completed in 2013. This plan was intended to help guide a major project to repair the vulnerable remains of the old cathedral of St Michael, and to conserve and interpret the country's largest collection of loose medieval glass and place it on display. The project will also review and advise on the long-term future of the ruins of St Michael's, a place of interlinked spiritual, symbolic, historic and architectural significance.

2. Origins and historical background

The origins of St Michael's are obscure, as elusive as the beginnings of the town of Coventry itself. The chapel of St Michael is first documented in the twelfth century, but the date of construction of the earliest building is not known. The foundation of the chapel and its subsequent evolution into a parish church can only be understood in relation to its immediate environment and the other churches that stood in its vicinity. It is a noteworthy aspect of Coventry's history that it was not divided into a large number of parishes, as in other medieval towns. As a consequence, St Michaels's and the other parish church, Holy Trinity, grew far larger than the average town church.

The churches before St Michael's

Sometime in the 1020s or 1030s Leofric, count of Mercia, and his wife, the Countess Godiva (*Godifu*), founded an abbey on the site of the ruins of the cathedral and of the priory of St Mary on Priory Row in the centre of Coventry. The church of Holy Trinity, on the south side of Priory Row, was recorded nearly a century later. Around the turn of the twelfth century the abbey church, dedicated to the Virgin Mary, was elevated to cathedral status when Bishop Robert Limesey transferred his see from Chester (moved there from Lichfield some 25 years earlier) to Coventry. From that time onwards the bishop functioned as the titular abbot of St Mary's and the abbey became a priory, under the governance of a prior.

It is unlikely that Bishop Limesey would have transferred the see from Chester if Coventry were only a village. The Domesday Book (1086) entry for Coventry, however, records only an agricultural community, which was assumed to be the case until 1976, when it was compellingly argued that the eleventh-century town, in common with others such as London and Winchester, had been omitted from the Domesday survey. The urban settlement probably formed the core of a separate abbey lordship, carved out of the large Coventry estate belonging to Leofric

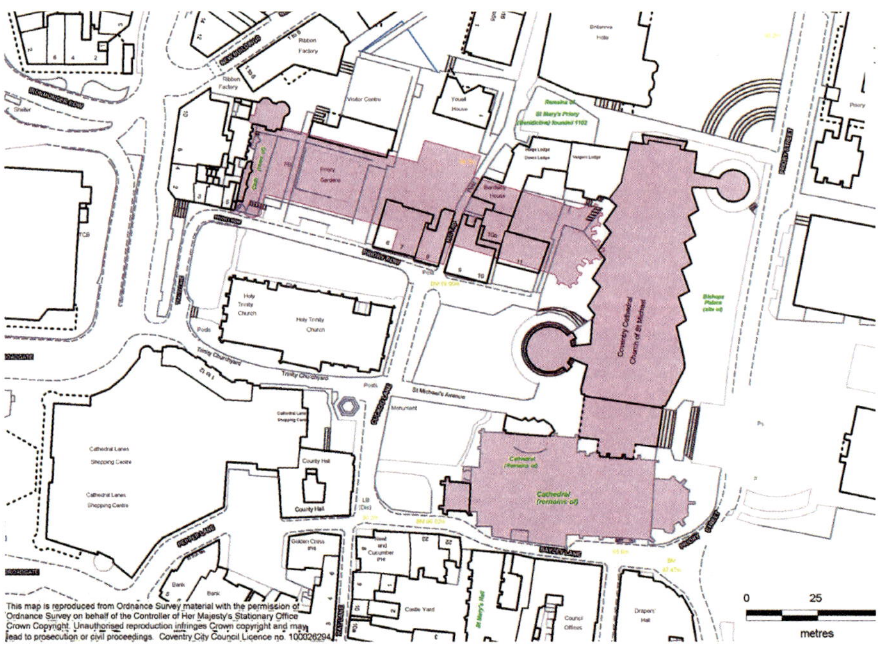

The outline of Coventry's three cathedrals is shown imposed on today's street pattern; they form a unique assemblage

Holy Trinity, the church of the Prior's Half, may have originated as an Anglo-Saxon minster

(d. 1057) and Godiva (d. 1067?). The Domesday Book only describes their rural estate under the name of the deceased Countess Godiva, then held by an agent on behalf of the king. This was granted to the earls of Chester in about 1100 and became known as the Earl's Half. At about the same time the abbey was re-designated a priory and its estate acquired the name the Prior's Half.

Although Holy Trinity, the church of the Prior's Half, is first mentioned in 1113, recent research into Coventry in the Anglo-Saxon period has suggested that it originated as a minster church as early as the seventh or early eighth century and was, therefore, much older than the church of St Michael. If true, this helps to explain why the eleventh-century abbey church of St Mary and its buildings were constructed to the north of Holy Trinity, on the less convenient sloping side of a hill. The summit of the hill may already have been occupied by Holy Trinity, necessitating the more unusual north cloister orientation when the priory was reconstructed in the twelfth century.

The creation of the earl's estate, the castle and the earl's chapel

It is not known whether the earls of Chester immediately set about developing a town on receiving Godiva's estate. They certainly built a castle, which was in existence by the 1140s when it was the scene of a bloody siege during the civil wars between Stephen and Matilda. The construction of the castle, most likely in the form of a motte and bailey, is fundamental in understanding the origins of St Michael's church and the topographical environment in which it grew. As a result of the subsequent obliteration of the castle above ground, its position is not obvious but recent research has narrowed its location. The castle ditch, which appears in thirteenth-century deeds as the back boundary of burgage (town) plots between Earl Street and Bayley Lane, is now considered to be the southern defence. The 'Castle Bakehouse' plot, the present Castle Yard, lies to the north of this projected line. It is probable that the east-west section of the present Bayley Lane directly reflects the position of an oval Norman bailey, running along its longitudinal axis.

If Bayley Lane cuts the former castle bailey roughly in half, then it follows that at least part of the present St Michael's church, which stands on the north side of Bayley Lane, must lie in the northern half of the former defensive enclosure. The north section of the castle ditch probably passes through much of the ruins. Given that the present footprint of the church, one of the largest in England, is likely to contain the site of its earliest building (a feature of many medieval churches) it would not be unreasonable to assume that this was constructed within the castle bailey. All this leads to the conclusion that St Michael's originated as a castle chapel, built for the personal use of the earls of Chester, a lord's private foundation, and which, like many others, came to function as a parish church.

While the first St Michael's served as a private chapel, the existing minster church of Holy Trinity could have continued to serve both the Earl's and the Prior's Half. The earl's extensive estate was mostly rural at this time. Holy Trinity stood on the west side of the large cemetery shared with the abbey church, which after 1100 became the cathedral of St Mary. This cemetery was an important feature of

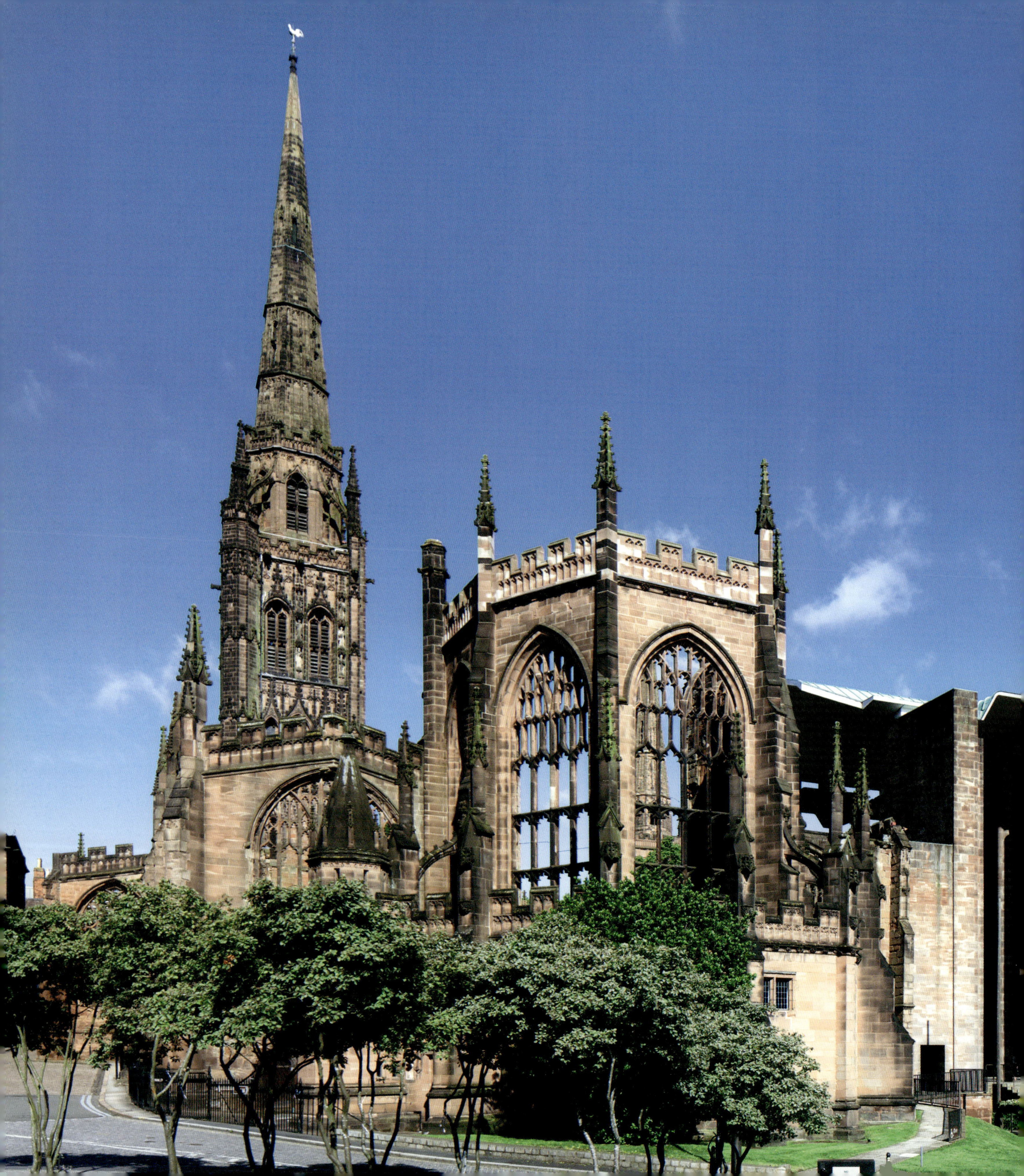

The new Coventry Cathedral, designed by Sir Basil Spence and built in a similar mellow sandstone to its predecessor, adjoins old St Michael's to the north

Bayley Lane originated as a new street running through the bailey of the demolished twelfth-century Norman castle

Coventry's early medieval topography and it is significant that it lay on the boundary between the two Halves.

In 1144 Earl Ranulf II of Chester, who had supported Empress Matilda's during the civil war, lost Coventry castle to the forces of King Stephen. It remained in the king's hands until 1154 when Ranulf's estates, including Coventry, were restored to him by Henry II. It appears that the castle was then abandoned as a fortification and the land made available for redevelopment, sometime at the end of the twelfth century. The largest surviving structure, the earl's chapel, could now play its part, fusing the earl's new town onto the prior's existing urban community. The chapel was conveniently available to be converted from private to parochial use.

The emergence of St Michael's as a parish church

During the period from the end of the ninth to the twelfth century the network of parishes as we know it was created. Most local churches originated as seigneurial foundations, the initiative of either lay or ecclesiastical lords. The Anglo-Saxon minster system was replaced by the parochial system, in which a single priest served a local community, often based upon the manor.

The earliest documented reference to St Michael's church is a charter of Earl Ranulf II, dated to 1153, in which he restored to Prior Lawrence and the monastery the 'chapel of saint Michael in my fee' and all other chapels that had been established in the remainder of his Coventry estates. Against the background of the great campaign of seigneurial church building, Ranulf still gave away or 'restored' all his new foundations to the monks of St Mary's, masters of the old minster church. The new parochial system was still in a state of flux, stirred by the inevitable conflicts that arose between the old and new ecclesiastical order. St Mary's would have rigorously defended its old rights and even managed to gain control of the chapels in the Earl's Half. By this time, however, pastoral care here was no longer administered by Holy Trinity alone, but also through St Michael's, its near neighbour serving the earl's new town, and a number of dependent rural chapels.

The process by which ecclesiastical authority over St Michael's passed to the priory took many more years. As late as 1182–84 the administrators of the young Ranulf III's estates granted an annual sum to the clerks of the earl's chapel of Coventry. Between 1190 and 1194 the same Ranulf III granted the tithes from his entire lands in Coventry to Ralph, his chaplain 'in the chapel of St Michael'.

A charter of 1183–84 provides the first information on the new chapels that had been founded in close proximity to one other in the centre of the growing town of Coventry. The priory cathedral of St Mary was in possession of the dependent chapels of Holy Trinity and the new foundation of Holy Cross 'situated in the cemetery'. The chapel of St Michael was recorded with its dependent rural chapels all lying on the rural parts of the earl of Chester's estates, but with the new chapel of St Mary 'in the cemetery of Coventry church [the priory cathedral]'. It is of major significance that only the dependent chapel of St Mary, and not St Michael's, shared the common cemetery with Holy Trinity and the chapel of the Holy Cross.

Today St Michael's church lies in its own burial ground, although part of this has been given up for the new cathedral. In the late twelfth century it is likely that it stood within the former castle, overlooking the cemetery to the north, which contained its dependent chapel of St Mary. It would appear that the prior had granted St Michael's burial rights within the existing common cemetery and promoted the construction of St Mary's, probably for use as a mortuary chapel. Although the castle's condition at the end of the twelfth century is unknown, it is likely that it was no longer actively defended. As an 'open' site, its chapel may have been accessible to the inhabitants of the earl's new town.

The location of the castle chapel helps explain the contrast in later urban topography between the south side and the north side of the church. From about 1200, former castle land was made available for building, including the north side of the new Bayley Lane. The result was that as the church expanded over the following three centuries, it came up against buildings already established on its west, south-west, south and south-east sides. The thirteenth-century south porch and later fifteenth-century aisle chapels, however, managed to establish a street frontage onto Bayley Lane. The church's expansion northwards was not so restricted and took place at the expense of the cemetery, particularly in the massive enlargements of the fifteenth century.

By the turn of the fourteenth century, the chapel of St Mary had been rebuilt and possibly relocated. It was known as 'the chapel of the Blessed Mary on the hill in the cemetery' and was the only obstacle to further extension northwards in the fifteenth century (see p.35 *et seq*).

Plan showing the position of the chapel of St Michael's within the presumed location of the castle bailey, and a possible adjustment of the boundary between the Earl's and Prior's Half following the rebuilding of St Michael's as a parish church, c.1250

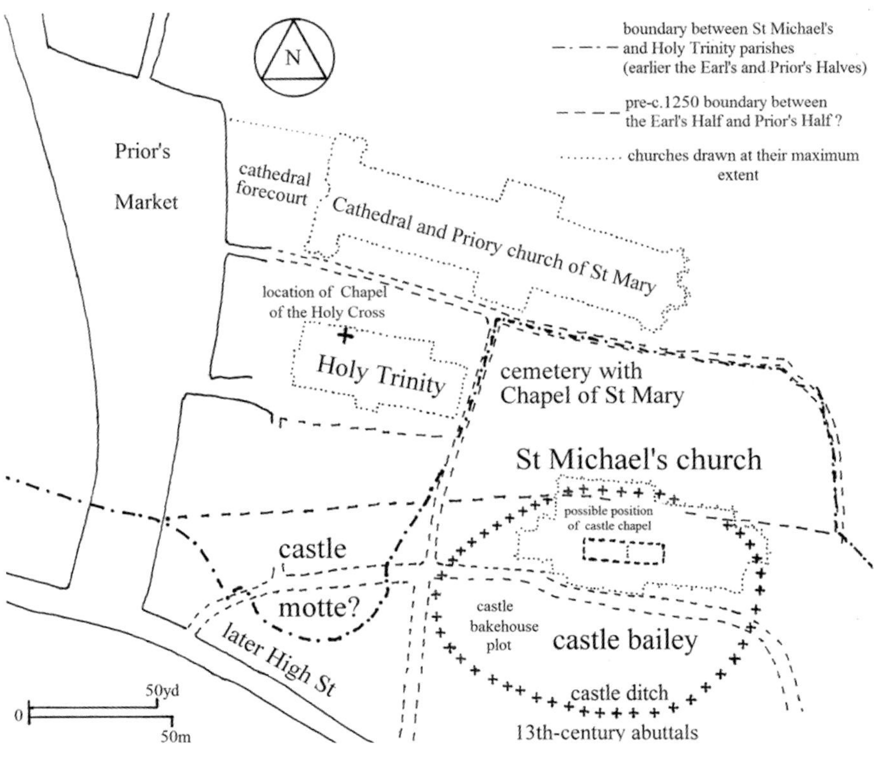

The west end of St Michael's: there was no room for the church to expand here as buildings had been constructed in the old castle bailey. To the north lay the old communal graveyard, still partly an open area today but much of it taken up by the new cathedral

RIGHT: *The huddle of buildings south of Bayley Lane was once replicated on the north side, limiting the potential for the church to expand southwards*

BELOW: *Plan showing St Michael's and its adjoining built-up area from the medieval period to the eighteenth century*

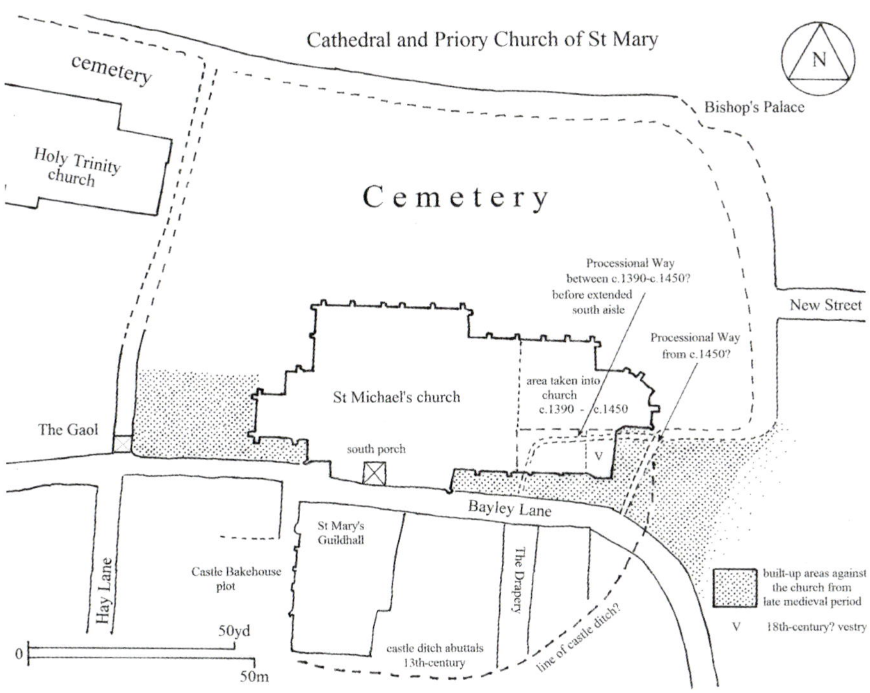

The battle for the parochial rights of St Michael's continued intermittently through the first half of the thirteenth century, with the monks appealing to the popes in Rome. The king and the bishop of Coventry also entered the fray and it was not until 1248 that a settlement was finally reached; the bishop recognised the priory's right to St Michael's, including its dependent chapels and its revenues. A vicarage was established for the first time and matters were further formalised in 1249.

The priory's victory in the century-long conflict was of great significance in the history of St Michael's church. In 1250 the priory acquired a large part of the earl's fee from Roger and Cecily de Montalt, who had succeeded to the earldom of Chester in Coventry. The Earl's Half and the Prior's Half were effectively united, with the prior now in control of a single lordship of Coventry, with each Half preserved as a parish to be served by St Michael's and Holy Trinity respectively. More importantly for St Michael's, its new ownership made possible the transformation of a small seigneurial chapel into a sizeable parish church.

3. From castle chapel to parish church

The twelfth-century chapel

There are no visible remains of the Norman Romanesque castle chapel, but an attempt can be made to establish its early form. In 1928 Philip Chatwin placed the chapel within the present nave, aligned with the two eastward projections from the tower. It is reasonable to assume that they represented the width of both the Romanesque and the Early English Gothic naves. The present nave is now wider through the later absorption of a north aisle. The only surviving Norman Romanesque church in Coventry, at Wyken, serves as a model with its common two-cell form of nave and chancel. The internal width of its nave happens to be close to the assumed width of the early St Michael's (c. 15ft, 4.5m).

The position of the chapel east-west is less easy to determine. Chatwin places it entirely within the present nave and twists the axis of its chancel a few degrees to the north to conform to the alignment of the surviving west crypt of c. 1300. Invisible from the nave today, this lies below the inner north aisle. This deviation of the crypt is only apparent when drawn on plan, as the present nave is set out on a straight line. An obvious twist to the north can be seen farther east in the misalignment of the fifteenth-century nave and chancel, still visible in the stubs of the piers that march across the floor of the ruins. It was even more obvious in the pre-Blitz church, as photographs and paintings demonstrate.

At present we cannot know whether the castle chapel had a break in its axis, or whether the alignment of the west crypt is relevant. The matter can only be proved when significant areas of the cathedral floor are archaeologically excavated. It would not be unusual to seek the location of the Norman

The first attempt to phase the development of St Michael's, by Philip Chatwin, 1928

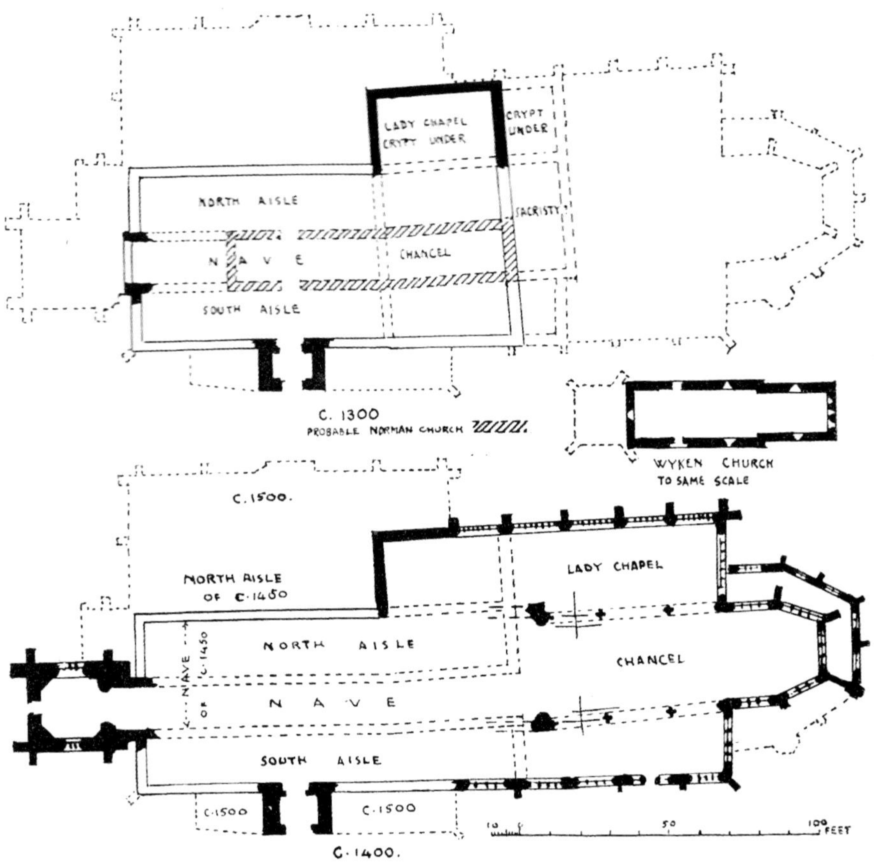

This fine interior of St Michael's by David Gee, 1862, clearly shows the misalignment of the fifteenth-century nave and chancel

chapel within the footprint of the much-expanded late medieval church.

It is also logical to position the chapel in the nave of St Michael's, where the terrain is level, rather than farther eastwards where the land outside the church begins to slope noticeably downwards. The consistent level throughout the interior of the cathedral today is entirely artificial.

The thirteenth-century church

The prior of St Mary's probably set about rebuilding St Michael's in the new Early English Gothic style soon after he became lord of the whole of Coventry in 1250. Much, if not all, of the Norman nave and chancel was demolished to construct north and south aisles. Little is left of the prior's church above ground except the south-east door, which provided

The mid-thirteenth-century south porch is the earliest surviving part of St Michael's. The doorway is flanked by engaged columns in Early English Gothic style and above it is a great trefoiled arch, which is unlikely to have been glazed originally. The south porch would once have been the most important entrance, opposite the Guildhall; it retains a tierceron rib vault from c.1300

This phase plan shows the development of St Michael's parish church c.1100–c.1500

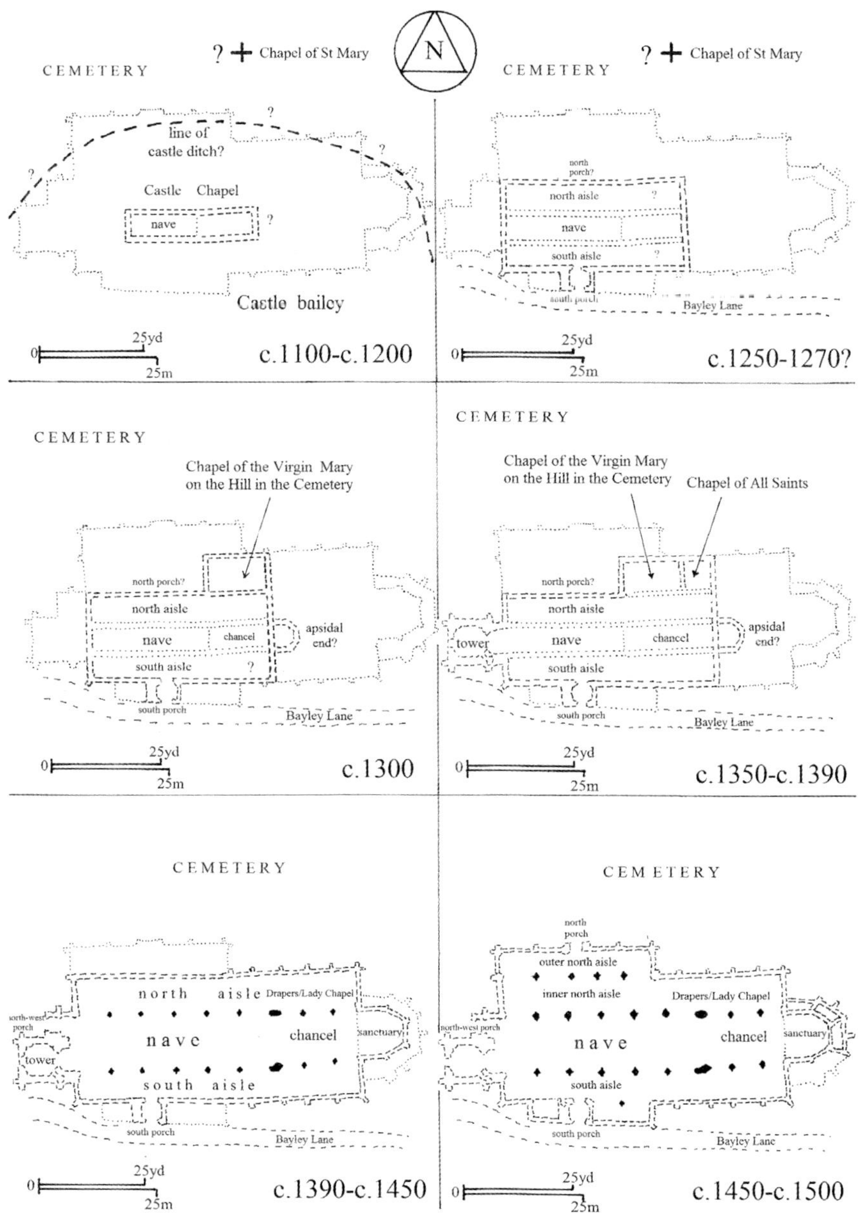

an entrance directly from Bayley Lane, and perhaps parts of the south aisle walls. A prominent trefoiled arch in the door proclaims the new style and scale of church building. The porch has been dated to the original phase of Gothic construction, but a tierceron rib vault within the porch appears to have been inserted in about 1300. The nave was probably extended westwards and the present west wall of the south aisle may delineate the position of the new west end. It is not known if a tower was constructed at this time. The thirteenth-century north aisle no longer exists, having been absorbed into a wider nave in the fifteenth century.

The appropriation of St Michael's church by the priory in 1249 provided the opportunity not only to build a new parish church, but also to divide the old communal cemetery belonging to St Mary's into two separate burial grounds, one attached to St Michael's and the other to Holy Trinity. The division of the cemetery is most likely to have taken place in the half century after 1250 and may have caused the redrawing of the parish boundaries. Later evidence confirms that St Michael's parish included the cemetery immediately north of the church, divided from the portion remaining with Holy Trinity by the present Cuckoo Lane. It is possible that there was an exchange of land, the salient of St Michael's cemetery projecting northwards being matched by a southwards extension of Holy Trinity parish in the vicinity of the present County Hall (see p. 21).

Two adjacent crypts (east and west) situated beneath the north side of the church survived the destructive fire of 14 November 1940. Their doorways can be seen on the right-hand side of the steps that descend from the old to the new cathedral. Convention has it that the larger west crypt was constructed about the year 1300, based on a copy of a grant of indulgences to be found in the records of the Drapers' Company, which later appropriated the chapel:

> 700 Indulgencies for 720 days, for building the Chapple & Charnell house of St Michael, Coventry, dated at Rome, the 8 year of Pope Boniface (Anno 1300)

It is likely that around 1300 a two-storey structure was constructed with a chapel dedicated to the

Virgin Mary above and a charnel house or ossuary in a crypt below. By the end of the thirteenth century the portion of ancient graveyard newly attached to St Michael's was probably full, creating the need for a place to store bones disturbed by grave-digging. The two-storey building also replaced the Norman twelfth-century chapel of St Mary, the site of which remains unknown. In the expansion of the church in the fifteenth century, most of the chapel above the charnel house (west crypt) was demolished and its space incorporated into a new north aisle.

The surviving 2 x 3 bay crypt, supported on two octagonal piers, has been dated architecturally to c. 1300, supporting the evidence of the indulgences. It would have appeared freestanding when first constructed, except on its south side, where it may have been attached to the main body of St Michael's via a chancel aisle. The north elevation of the charnel house contained a door in the centre bay, flanked by two high windows. The two-bay east elevation was also lit by two windows. Access to the first-floor chapel was presumably provided by an external staircase, probably rising on the west side, where there are no windows in the elevation of the present crypt. The two-storey building would have been a prominent feature of the cemetery, rising high over the falling ground to the north-east and east, such that the description *'super monte'*, 'on the hill', was added to the original dedication to the Virgin Mary.

The earliest known reference to the 'chapel on the hill' can be dated to soon after 1317. John Le Vineter

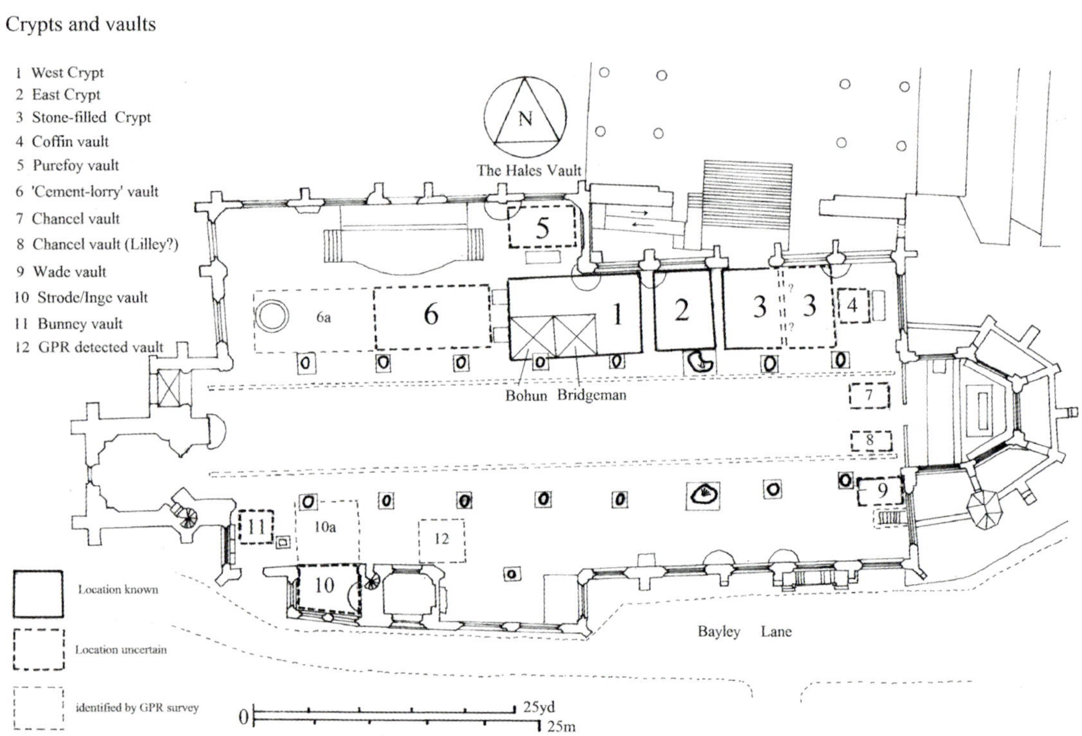

ABOVE: *The door to the smaller east crypt, one of two adjacent crypts on the north side of the church which survived the fire of 1940*

LEFT: *Location plan of the known crypts and burial vaults within St Michael's; there are many more to be discovered*

The west crypt of c.1300, the surviving part of the 'chapel of the Virgin Mary on the hill in the cemetery' which once stood above it. This view looks westwards; the north wall on the right once faced directly onto to the cemetery

(the vintner) granted 12d rent per annum to pay for a light to be maintained in the 'Chapel of the Blessed Virgin Mary on the Hill in the cemetery of St Michael'. Interestingly the chapel was also distinguished by its location in the cemetery into which it projected. It should not be identified with the present Drapers' Chapel, earlier known as the Lady Chapel, situated in the north aisle of the chancel and through which today the new cathedral is entered from the old. This aisle was only completed in the great rebuilding campaign of the first half of the fifteenth century. Two fourteenth-century wall paintings were discovered in 1941 when some masonry collapsed at the corner of the Girdlers' Chapel and the Drapers'/Lady Chapel (see p.43). It is likely that these were executed within the chapel upper storey, proving that not all of this level was demolished in the fifteenth century.

ABOVE LEFT: *A capital detail from the west crypt; between each of eight ribs rising from the two octagonal piers is a sharp pyramidal 'spur' to effect a neater transition onto the capital*
ABOVE RIGHT: *The north wall of the west crypt, which contained a door leading directly to the cemetery. Its blocked arch can be seen above the more recent doorway*

The fourteenth century: tower, spire and the chapel of All Saints

During the fourteenth century Coventry emerged as one of the most important towns in medieval England and its merchants and tradesmen used some of the fruits of their commercial success to establish chantries within St Michael's. Priests were paid to sing (chant) masses at the altars of their founders to reduce any time spent by them or their families in Purgatory. At least three chantries are known to have been created in the fourteenth century: Merington's Chantry in 1323, Shepey's in 1330 and Haye's in 1388. With only two aisles available for them, demand soon outgrew the space available.

The priory's lordship of Coventry lasted for only a century, the town's leading citizens wishing to be free of its authority. Aided by Queen Isabella, wife of Edward II, they eventually received a royal charter of incorporation in 1345, which created a new independent governing body headed by a mayor. In the 'Tri-partite' agreement of 1355 the prior was forced to acknowledge his much diminished role in Coventry's affairs. The priory, however, retained the advowson (the right to select a vicar) of St Michael's until the sixteenth-century dissolution of religious houses.

The combination of the town's growing wealth and its citizens' freedom of action explains the decision to build an enormously ambitious tower and spire, which in the medieval period were only surpassed in height by Salisbury and Norwich. Work on the tower began in the early 1370s in an area where large secular buildings had already been completed. In the 1340s the Guildhall of St Mary was constructed on the opposite side of Bayley Lane to St Michael's. Here Coventry's new urban oligarchy, some of its richest merchants, met for religious ceremonial, feasting and mutually beneficial trading networks. In the same decade a new Drapery, one of the largest cloth markets in the country, was established east of the Guildhall, stretching along the line of St Mary's Street from Bayley Lane to Earl Street. In 1392 the guilds of St Mary, St John the Baptist, the Holy Trinity and St Katherine amalgamated to form the Trinity Guild, and St Mary's Guildhall was rebuilt and extended.

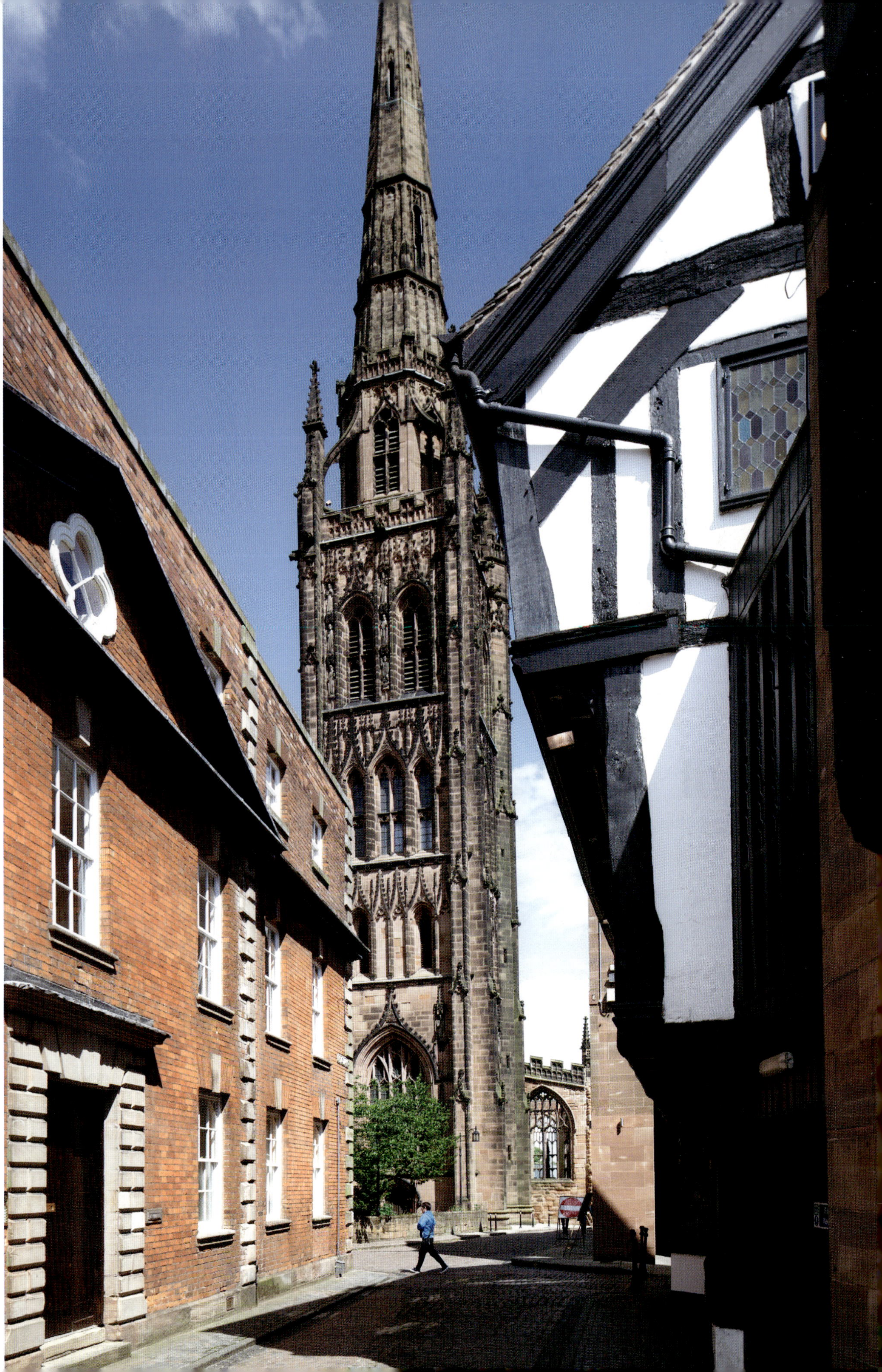

The magnificent tower and spire, built c.1375–c.1450; no other medieval parish church spire surpassed this in height and only two cathedrals, Salisbury and Norwich, matched it

FAR LEFT: The east side of the tower reveals the position of an earlier roof, showing as a low-pitched angle of inserted stone. The later higher roof caused damage to the windows and blind arcading of the first stage of the tower

LEFT: When the tower was first built it respected the width of the thirteenth-century nave, represented by the two wall stubs that project from it. The great rebuilding of the church from the 1390s to c.1450 created a wider nave to the north, hence the window and doorway immediately to the right

It is no surprise, therefore, that a powerful merchant family should fund an ecclesiastical building project that would not only reflect its own wealth and prestige, but also that of Coventry. The traditional view is that the brothers Adam and William Botoner funded the construction of the tower in 1372, but the City Annals, a year-by-year contemporary summary of main events, record two other dates, 1374 and 1375. Some, but not all, of the versions also record a 20- or 21-year building campaign and a cost of £100 per annum. Curiously, the tower, although massive, relates to the width of the narrower twelfth and thirteenth-century naves (see plans on pp. 24 and 27), which suggests that it was not conceived as part of the greater plan to rebuild the whole church, beginning in the 1390s, but as an edifice in its own right. Consequently it would have been singularly out of scale with the thirteenth-century church; the Botoners may have been keener on building big than on compliance with any architectural aesthetics. If the tower had been conceived as part of the great rebuilding, then it would almost certainly have been placed in a central position against the west wall of the widened nave.

That the tower was constructed as a freestanding building with its own buttresses and only later connected by a short section of wall to the narrower thirteenth-century nave, is also suggested by the presence of a straight joint in the south stub wall that projects from the east side of the tower. One version of the Annals states that 'William and Adam Botoner built St Michael's steeple to the battlements and then died. The church body and 2 side aisles were built before', confirming that the tower was erected at the west end of a pre-existing nave and pair of aisles.

More difficult to explain is the mark of a low-pitched roof line on the east face of the tower, lower than the roof destroyed in the Blitz. A steeply-pitched roof would be expected on a thirteenth-century church. Low-pitched roofs were introduced in the latter part of the fourteenth century but were still comparatively rare at this time. The evidence left in the stonework of the tower indicates that this was the position of the roof when the tower was built, between the 1370s and 1390s. It is sufficiently high to have accommodated a clerestory below and the implication is that an earlier thirteenth-century roof had already been removed and rebuilt at a higher level to allow more light into the nave. This probably took place at the same time as the construction of the tower and, if so, this was one of the earliest examples of a low-pitched leaded roof in England.

RIGHT: *A pair of slim and elegant flying buttresses from each of the tower corner pinnacles help support the octagon and its spire above*
BELOW: *This 1909 engraving of the east side of the tower shows the earlier roof position and the later roof over the wider nave destroyed in the Blitz; note how it intercepts the windows of the tower*

It was only to survive for half a century or so. The plan for a much wider nave was probably conceived as the tower was being completed in the 1390s. The decision to remove an expensive and fashionable roof within so short a time speaks eloquently of the self-confidence and soaring ambition of the church's affluent parishioners.

At about the same time that the tower and roof of the church were being constructed, an extension dedicated to All Saints was added to the east side of the chapel of St Mary on the Hill (see plan on p. 24). The evidence is the papal petition of 1449–50 in which the drapers of Coventry sought to re-endow their new chapel of St Mary and All Saints with all the land and privileges that the former 'two contiguous chapels, one of St Mary the Virgin, the other of All Saints' enjoyed. The document provides an identity for the two surviving contiguous crypts, that on the west being the lower storey or charnel house of St Mary, that on the east the charnel house for the new chapel of All Saints.

Compared to the west crypt, the All Saints charnel house is more crudely constructed and a third smaller (2 x 1 bays). The ribs of the vault have a much sharper profile than those in the west crypt, with deep chamfers, and have been dated to the second half of the fourteenth century. On the north side facing the cemetery (now the new cathedral) is a door and a window. Two windows used to light the east elevation, repeating the original arrangement of the west crypt, whose windows now give onto the interior of the All Saints' crypt or charnel house. The new crypt floor was not excavated into the bed rock as deeply as in the west crypt, resulting in a lower vaulted space. The lower springing points of the vault ribs, without corbels, required the removal of part of the plinth of the original external wall of the west crypt. The dedication to All Saints (All Hallows)

The east crypt, dating from c.1350; it was the charnel house to the chapel of All Saints that once stood above, and was converted into a chapel in the following century with stairs, approached by the doorway, inserted at the far end (now blocked) to provide direct access to the church above

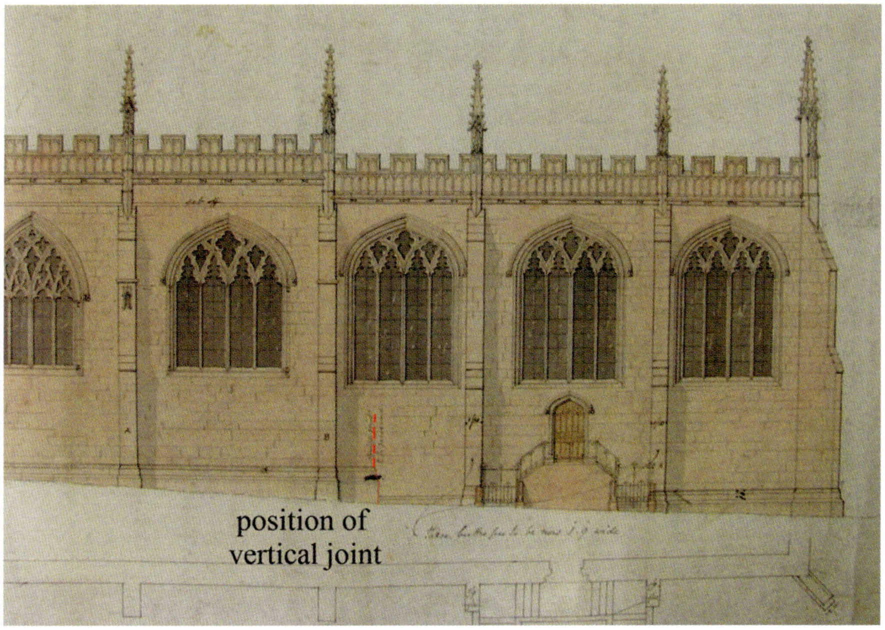

ABOVE: *J. Drayton Wyatt's south elevation of 1853; his intention to retain the important vertical joint in the exterior repairs has been highlighted in red*
BELOW RIGHT: *The vertical joint today, as seen from Bayley Lane*

was significant, as it was the feast day commonly associated with the remembrance of the dead, celebrated on 1 November, followed by All Souls on 2 November.

A vertical joint in the exterior south wall of the south aisle overlooking Bayley Lane in the bay to the left of the steps probably indicates the termination of the aisle at this time. It is no coincidence that this position aligns with the eastern end of the All Saints crypt on the north side of the church. It is possible that a Lady Chapel projected farther eastwards from the thirteenth-century chancel.

The fifteenth century: the great rebuilding

The poignant remains of the great body of St Michael's church are almost entirely a product of the great rebuilding campaign of the fifteenth century. In the 1390s, with the tower complete, work began on a new apsidal east end, constructed well beyond the east end of the thirteenth- and fourteenth-century church. An entirely new plan was implemented, which not only doubled the width of the nave and chancel, but also extended the church by about another third (to c.280ft, 85.3.m, including the tower and vestries). The misalignment of nave and chancel has already been noted and is found in many churches. The idea, beloved of the Victorians, that saw the inclination as the tilting of Christ's head to the left (his right) on the cross can be dismissed. In reality, as many chancels incline right as left, and the material world of topography and landownership generally explain such deviations.

It is possible that the angle of the chancel and apse at St Michael's was influenced by physical constraints, perhaps the alignment of a road or a property boundary, but this cannot be proved. Between 1672 and 1674 a narrow range of buildings which had stood against part of the south nave aisle and the whole of the south chancel aisle, and opposite the north door of the Drapery on Bayley Lane, was demolished. This had originated as stables and was replaced by six shops in around 1480. It is possible that the plot on which they were built was originally longer and that its rear boundary influenced the alignment of the new chancel. The site now coincides with the wider section of the carriageway on Bayley Lane, opposite the opening of St Mary Street. Next to these buildings and to the east, there was a gap in the buildings lining the north side of Bayley Lane as it gradually curved southwards. This was the start of the Processional Way that encircled the church from at least the early fifteenth century (see plan on p. 23). It was claimed in the late fifteenth century that the south chancel aisle was built upon its earlier course.

Whatever the state and status of the land used for the new apse and chancel, the extension of the church to a length of about 280ft (85.3m) on a sloping site would have required a major build-up of material to maintain a level floor from west to east. This can be best seen in the polygonal apse, which stands high above the surrounding ground, as if on

a terrace, and along Bayley Lane, where the cathedral floor remains level as the road gradually falls. The eastern half of the cathedral floor must therefore consist mainly of made-up ground, while the original medieval surface lies buried well below.

The rebuilding of St Michael's was an exceptional project, providing a model for other large parish churches during the remainder of the century. The polygonal apse is outstanding, both architecturally and in its rarity. Each of the five sides was almost filled with glazing set in Perpendicular tracery in a huge two-centred arch. These dazzling windows were always seen against the sky owing to the steep fall in the land below.

Earlier buildings with apsidal ends are known locally, the closest in date and style to St Michael's being the chapter house at St Mary's, Warwick, and the hall and lodgings at Kenilworth Castle, both the work of secular lords. The chancel of the earl of Warwick's church, started c.1367, and the east end and cloister of Gloucester Cathedral have also been identified as probable sources of inspiration for the form of the elevations. These close parallels help to define a possible date range for the chancel and apse of c.1390–c.1420. The west end of the chancel was marked by a massive pair of piers, both containing a spiral staircase ascending to the rood screen, but only the north giving access to the roof. In the

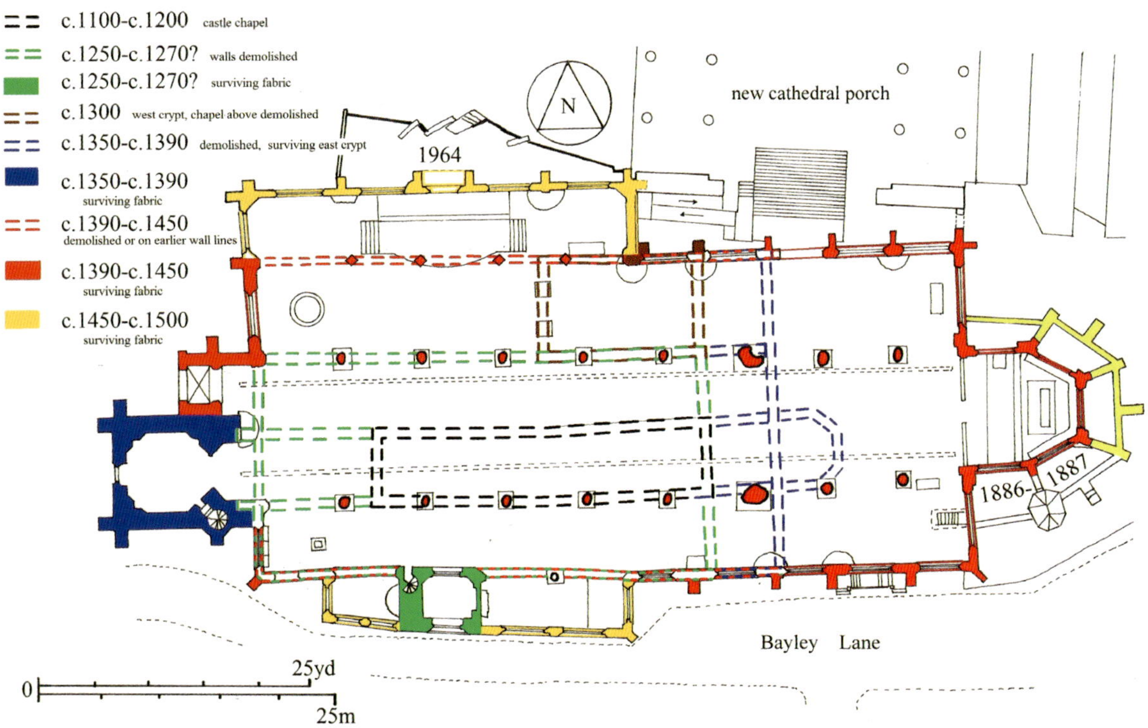

ABOVE: The polygonal apse, c.1390–c.1420, rises high above the historic land level in Bayley Lane and marks the church's expansion way beyond the confines of the original castle chapel. This was the first part to be built in the Perpendicular Gothic style

LEFT: Composite phase plan of the development of St Michael's

OPPOSITE: Looking east through the apse to open sky

The five windows of the apse soar loftily above the charred cross behind the altar. They are 'sub-arcuated', divided into two subordinate arches, and their height gives room for several stages of both ogee and two-centred arches, the latter emphasised by horizontal transoms

BELOW: *The misalignment of chancel and nave is seen most clearly in the left (north) side pier stumps, the largest, the third from the apse, marking the division between two parts. They were also more massive to accommodate a spiral staircase*

BELOW RIGHT: *The construction of the wider nave was resolved at the west end by the creation of a new porch and window above. The angle on the crenellation represents the new roof line*

absence of a chancel arch, the piers helped emphasise the important change from chancel to nave and belonged architecturally to the nave.

The construction of the new nave would logically follow that of the chancel and has been dated to between the 1430s and the late 1440s, although there is a clear architectural continuity. The west porch alongside the tower by which the nave is entered must also date from this period. It aligns with the former thirteenth-century north aisle. The arches of the nave arcade were four-centred and wider than the two-centred arches in the chancel. All the clerestory windows were four-centred and paired in each bay with traceried wall panels below. A new low-pitched timber roof stretched higher and wider than its predecessor, requiring the removal of moulded stonework around two existing windows and the blind arcading of the second stage on the tower, still visible today.

The completion of the octagonal belfry on the tower is dated to about 1430, when bells were first hung in the steeple, and work on the spire began in 1444. The tower stands to about 131ft 8in (40.1m) and the addition of the octagonal belfry (30ft 9in, 9.3m) and the spire of about 125ft 9in (38.3m) and assumed weathercock (7ft 6in, 2.2m) raised the height of the whole to nearly 296ft (90.2m), by coincidence a little over the length of the completed church including the tower base.

The 1449–50 papal petition provides a date by which most of the great rebuilding was completed. The removal of most of the original upper storeys of the chapels of St Mary and All Saints probably took place in two stages. The smaller chapel of All Saints over the present east crypt had to be demolished first to make way for the north staircase pier and the north aisle behind, but some of its masonry may have been retained in the new north wall. A staircase, now blocked at cathedral floor level and leading down into the east crypt, was probably constructed

The interior of the roofless cathedral is now the best place to appreciate the loftiness and architectural virtuosity of tower and spire. As a result of the widening of the nave, the tower now stands off-centre (to the left in this photograph). The nearest pier on the right represents the junction of the nave and chancel

visitor information

The octagon and spire were completed in the first half of the fifteenth century, reaching nearly 296ft (90.2m), the highest on any medieval parish church. The spire still dominates the skyline viewed at a distance both from within the city and beyond

at about the same time and the surviving aumbry and piscina were added to furnish a new crypt chapel. The ribs at the south end of the crypt now disappear into the wall supporting the staircase into which the aumbry and piscina are set. St Mary's Chapel, standing over what is now the west crypt, was probably next to be demolished and incorporated into the two easternmost bays of the new north aisle. A space was provided for the earlier dedications to St Mary and All Saints in the relatively new north chancel aisle.

The Trinity Guild appears to have taken possession of the east crypt or charnel house which originally lay beneath All Saints, converting it to a chapel assigned for burial rights and retaining the designation 'chapel on the hill' or more rarely 'chapel in the cemetery'. The guild had its own church-sized chapel of St John to provide for the living, which still stands at the east end of Spon Street. It retained an interest in St Michael's, simply because the ultimate destination of many of its members was a space below the floor of the church or in its graveyard.

The new Drapers' (originally Lady) Chapel was constructed high over the sloping ground to the east of the demolished chapels of St Mary and All Saints; sometime during the intervening period the Drapers had appropriated the former Lady Chapel. There was room below to construct a crypt, rather than making up the considerable amount of ground necessary to lay the floor level with the new chancel. This new crypt was not provided with windows and caused the blocking of the two eastward facing windows of the former All Saints charnel house. The north nave aisle interior was continued westwards from the new Drapers'/Lady Chapel through the site of the demolished 'chapel on the hill', finishing, as it does today, in line with the original west front of the thirteenth-century church. The exposure in March 1941 of a fourteenth-century wall painting of Christ, with the Madonna and Child below, on the corner between the Girdlers' Chapel (outer north aisle) and the Drapers'/Lady Chapel (inner north aisle) is strong evidence that some of the fabric of the 'chapel on the hill' was retained in the great rebuilding.

It is assumed that the south aisle began at the tower, as previously, and ran along both nave and chancel to terminate in a new east window. The continuation eastwards from the visible vertical joint,

The west crypt, showing the two aumbries (recesses protected by doors to store sacred vessels) and the piscina (the arched recess where the priest washed the vessels and his hands in a bowl)

ABOVE LEFT: *To the left of the present entrance to the new cathedral and beyond, the chapels of the Blessed Virgin on the Hill and All Saints were demolished to make way for the north aisle accommodating the new Lady Chapel or Drapers' Chapel*

BELOW FAR LEFT: *Wall painting, thought to show Christ and dating to c.1330, which was exposed in 1941, proving that not all the Chapel on the Hill was demolished for the new north aisle*

BELOW LEFT: *Copy of a painting of the Madonna and Child dating to c.1330 which was exposed by a fall of masonry in 1941 and has since been destroyed* indicating the termination of the fourteenth-century church (see p.35), was certainly constructed by 1480 when the 'Southe baye' was built over part of the Processional Way.

Although the church had not yet reached its maximum size, considerable extra space had already been made for new chapels, chantries and altars. Crosse's and Preston's Chantries are first recorded in 1412, during the major period of building work. Crosse's Chantry was eventually taken over by the Mercers' Company and must have been located in the south chancel aisle. There is considerable uncertainty over the location of many private devotional spaces; Preston's Chantry, for example, was established at the altar of Holy Trinity and the Blessed Virgin. Dedications to the Virgin Mary were popular and there may have been another altar besides that in the Drapers'/Lady Chapel.

It is not known whether the outer north and south aisles were part of the original plan for the great rebuilding. The dating is not yet certain and there is no agreement over the sequence of events, one authority suggesting that the outer north aisle, and therefore the great majority of the church, was completed by the time of the royal visit of Henry VI in 1451. This left only the guild chapels, the Cappers' and Dyers', forming the outer south aisle, to be built on either side of the south porch, probably by 1463.

In all likelihood, however, construction of the outer north aisle began soon after 1450 and was completed by 1500. This aisle gives every indication of being constructed at a different time to the north chancel aisle and there was certainly a north church door by 1495. The windows of the north chancel aisle have two-centred pointed arches while three of the north windows of the outer aisle by contrast are two-centred on the interior and incorporate flanking traceried stone panels. On the exterior, however, these stone panels are expressed as part of the ashlar wall, reducing the width of the windows, so that they appear, quite cleverly, as a four-centred arches. Only one of these windows is visible, the others hidden by the cathedral bookshop built in 1964.

The construction of the outer north aisle would have required the demolition of the original north aisle wall. The work involved the loss of expensive and relatively new fabric and would only have been undertaken in response to constant demand for

The south aisle of the chancel, with its three windows now devoid of tracery, was constructed by 1480 and diverted the Processional Way farther to the east

increased chapel space. The outer north aisle was constructed so that it obstructed two of the three bays of the north elevation of the west crypt. As a consequence, the centrally placed door, which had served the crypt since about 1300, was blocked, requiring the reconstruction of the window to the east as a replacement doorway. For the first time in its history the crypt was no longer lit by exterior windows.

The present north porch, or at least its spiral staircase, may have been an afterthought since it sits uncomfortably close to the window immediately west. The porch is a distinguished piece of late Perpendicular Gothic, its exterior unfortunately obscured by the cathedral bookshop. The spiral staircase on the west side, still visible today, led to an exterior door and a corbelled polygonal platform or pulpit under a steep crocketted canopy. The north porch and pulpit, facing the cemetery, may have had a specific funerary function. St Andrew's or the Smiths' Chapel has traditionally been placed between the north porch and the west window of the outer north aisle. There is some evidence to suggest that it was indeed located here after 1449.

After its rebuilding, completed around 1500, St Michael's ranked as one of the great urban churches of the late Middle Ages. The mercantile wealth of the city had been invested in an abundance of chapels, chantries and altars which divided the new aisles into private compartments, defined by intricately-carved timber screens (parcloses) and decorated with religious wall paintings, statues, and guild and company regalia and insignia. For all this the church needed the equivalent of four aisles, making

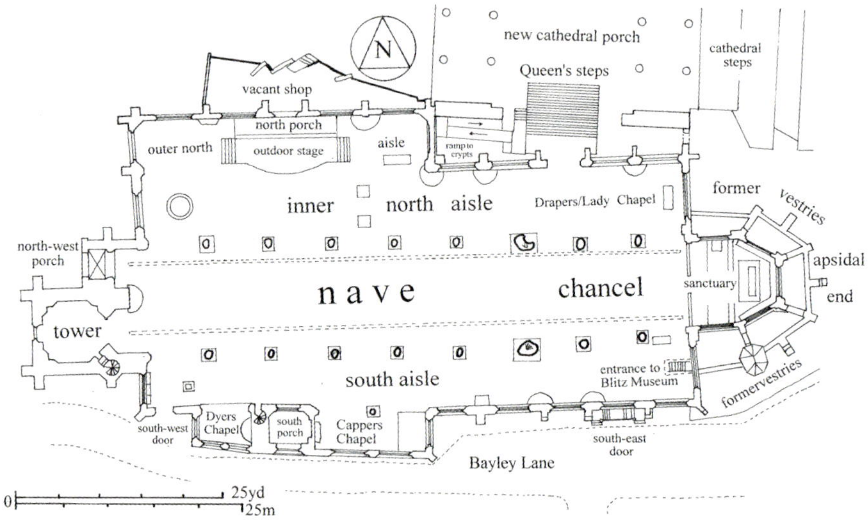

ABOVE: *Orientation plan of St Michael's at its full extent after rebuilding, with the new cathedral leading out of it to the north*

LEFT: *The east end of the Lady or Drapers' Chapel, under which lies a vault which may contain the remains of two of the Berkeley family of Caludon Castle, Coventry. The recumbent figure is of H.W. Yeatman-Biggs, the first post-Reformation bishop of Coventry (1918–1922)*

it one of the widest in the country. Stepping into the church on a major feast day, the visual senses would have been reinforced by the auditory and olfactory: the chanting of priests and ringing of bells, the vapours from burning wax and tallow candles and the smell of rushes and herbs scattered on the floor.

ABOVE: *The outer north aisle and north porch (c.1450–c.1500). The spiral staircase of the north porch sits uncomfortably close to the window on the left and may have been an afterthought. The windows, with their flanking blind panels, appear as two-centred pointed arches on the interior and four-centred arches on the exterior*
RIGHT: *The north porch as recorded by A.E. Everitt in 1847*

Colour would have poured into the building through the painted glass of the windows, displaying both religious subjects and the heraldic devices of the rich patrons who paid for them. The view to the high altar was obscured and public access denied by a carved timber screen on which rose a large crucifix flanked by statues of the Virgin Mary and John the Baptist. The rood or 'candle' beam supported a permanently burning light, while candles and tapers would have illuminated many of the chapels.

The interior of the church was also used as a space to accommodate mortal remains. The wealthiest families in the city could pay for the privilege of 'intramural' interment beneath the church floor, some in private vaults. The growth of the church throughout the medieval period provided more room for this type of burial, but by the sixteenth century a large area of the floor, including the nave and chancel, must have been densely packed with graves, each covered by a stone slab to form a continuous 'pavement'. Gravestones were often set with brass engravings; Coventry was a major centre of monumental brass production in the late fifteenth century. Commemorative brass plaques could also be fixed to the walls. The floors of guild or chantry chapels were usually reserved for members, sponsors or benefactors. There were also large funerary monuments. One tomb chest supported three recumbent

Looking eastward along the nave and chancel to the polygonal east end; the tracery is completely missing from the five windows on the right, owing to the ferocity with which the organ burned in the fire on the night of 14 November 1940

effigies; Elizabeth Swillington, who died in 1546, lay with her husbands on either side, one dressed in armour and the other in lawyers' robes. A number of other tomb chests were certainly in existence in the sixteenth century, including two for the Berkeley family of Caludon Castle (see p.55) and one for the draper Julius Nethermill (d.1539) and his wife.

In 1522 there were 25 priests, including the vicar, attached to St Michael's. Eighteen were either parochial chaplains or auxiliary clergy serving in the main parish church and six were identified as chantry priests. A large number of obits, endowments supporting priests to say prayers on specific days such as the anniversary of the benefactor's death, were distributed among the altars. In 1518 William Haddon, a draper, left money in his will to nine altars in St Michael's, including the Drapers'/Lady Chapel. There is no evidence for a medieval vicarage house, but it appears that some of the priests lived in chambers situated on the north side of Bayley Lane, near the apsidal east end of the church and facing the cemetery.

ABOVE: *The interior of the north porch, with a gallery above and the doorway arch below half-buried by a stone platform built in the ruins in the late 1940s*

LEFT: *The chest tomb of Lady Elizabeth Swillington (d.1546), with her first husband (d.1500) on the left and her second husband (d.1526) on the right; it was destroyed in the Blitz*

4. From parish church to cathedral

The dissolution of the religious guilds and chantries

Cataclysmic changes were brought about by the dissolution of the religious guilds and chantries under the Chantries Act of 1547 (Edward VI). This included an injunction against obits (prayers for the dead), reflecting the earlier official abolition of purgatory under the 1536 Act of the Ten Articles. Much of the space in St Michael's parish church therefore ceased to have a purpose and its many chantry priests and chaplains were evicted. The 1547 act also dissolved the Trinity Guild, based in St Mary's Guildhall. Although the guild represented a substantial part of Coventry's ruling merchant class and had a clear commercial goal, it could not escape the act; its support of regular, even daily, intercession for the dead, readily apparent in the great number of altars and serving priests in St Michael's and its own guild chapel of St John, made its religious purpose clear.

Little is known about the attitude of the parishioners of St Michael's to the reforms, or the extent to which they resisted or accepted the new religion. During the reign of Queen Mary (1554–58) there was a return to traditional ritual and the retrieval of hidden vestments and plate. From 1553 for four and a half years the church remained without a vicar, probably because of the small stipend. This situation was resolved in 1558. The accession of the determinedly Protestant Queen Elizabeth I in 1558 was followed by outbreaks of local iconoclasm. In 1560, according to the Annals, 'all images and Popish reliques [were] beaten down, and burnt in the street'. In 1569 the parish registers were destroyed 'by some who were eager to burn Popish Books, that they burned the Registers, because they had some marks of Popery in them'. It is likely that in these unstable times the internal appearance of the church began to deteriorate.

The last reference to the 'chapel on the hill' (the converted east crypt) dates to 1539, when a payment was made for mending a holy water basin standing at the chapel door. The Trinity Guild was responsible for its upkeep until the dissolution of 1547. The 'charnell house' in the cemetery, noted by John Leland on his visit to Coventry sometime between 1539 and 1543, was probably the west crypt.

The trading companies in Coventry managed to survive the dissolution of the religious guilds, as they were able to prove that their functions were primarily secular and commercial. Foremost was the Drapers' Company, which managed to retain property which had previously belonged to the 'Wardens of Our Lady's Rent in St Michael's'. The company continued to pay for tallow candles and wax and for the cleaning of their chapel in the north aisle up to the 1590s, and as late as 1599 they maintained a light on 'ye Rode Loft'. This confirms the survival of the rood screen up to this date, despite official disapproval of both screens and lights.

Located on the opposite side of the church to the Drapers' Chapel, the Mercers appear, at some time

The exterior of the Cappers' Chapel (early 1460s), projecting into Bayley Lane; the chapel, built later than the south aisle to the right, bears a high moulded plinth course

The Dyers' Chapel was originally a two-storey structure, each with its own tier of windows. The floor was removed in the nineteenth century and the windows rebuilt as one; two of the stone corbels that once supported the floor are visible in the photograph

unknown, to have taken over the part of the south chancel aisle previously occupied by St Katharine's altar and Crosse's Chantry (see plan on p.28). By 1579 the Mercers had handed over the maintenance of their chapel to the churchwardens, to whom they paid an annual fee. A similar arrangement was made with the Drapers in the 1590s.

The chapel of St Thomas was in existence by 1458. It is now identified with the later Cappers' Chapel flanking the east side of the south porch, which was constructed after the extension of the south aisle, perhaps in the early 1460s. According to the Annals, however, the chapel of St Thomas was founded by the Woollen Cardmakers in 1465. It is possible, therefore, that the chapel was moved to a new location in this year. In 1531 the Cardmakers gave up the chapel, owing to a large decline in membership, and it was taken over by the prospering Cappers' Fellowship. The chapel on the west side of the south porch seems to have always belonged to the Dyers' Company, the first reference to it being in 1463. It was built as a two-storey structure, with two tiers of windows, the upper one being the largest. The Smiths' Company occupied the west part of the outer north aisle, also known as St Andrew's Chapel. The eastern part of the aisle on the other side of the north porch was taken by the Girdlers' Company from 1564.

Shepey's Chantry, founded in 1330, was associated with the altar of St Laurence. The altar survived into the post-dissolution period and has traditionally been located immediately to the west of the Drapers' Chapel, on the evidence that in 1612 room was made

in St Laurence's Chapel to hang the fire buckets belonging to the Drapers' Company. The presence of so many company chapels in St Michael's meant that not all the chapels and altars were abandoned after the Edwardine reforms, so the church may not have presented a picture of complete desertion.

St Michael's was first and foremost a town church and was not dominated by a powerful aristocratic family. One of the few large manor houses in the immediate area of Coventry was Caludon Castle. In the sixteenth century this was owned by the Berkeley family, of Berkeley Castle in Gloucestershire, where their deceased were usually returned to be buried. In the case of Katherine, wife of Sir Henry Berkeley, an exception was made. She died at Caludon and on 20 May 1596 her funeral was held at St Michael's. She was 'interred in a vault in the northeast corner of that Church neare the drapers Chappell there'. In 1611 her son, Thomas, was buried 'within the same Iron Grate wherein his mother lyeth'. Each had a chest tomb placed in the Drapers' Chapel. Their location is confirmed in an engraving by Wenceslaus Hollar first published in 1656. As late as 1909 Lady Katherine's chest tomb stood just outside the Lady Chapel screen, but Thomas's had been moved to the west side of the north porch.

From the description of the burials, it would appear that the Berkeleys were interred within an existing vault, partitioned off with an iron grating for security. This vault may be the one that lies immediately to the east of the east crypt and is now filled with broken moulded stonework. With no external

Sketch of the tower, south door and Dyers' Chapel by J. Drayton Wyatt, early 1850s; note the two tiers of windows in the Dyers' Chapel to the right for the two storeys within, soon to be removed. It is not known when the south door was constructed. The external entrance to the tower spiral staircase can be seen behind the railing

RIGHT: *Wenceslaus Hollar's engraving from 1657 of the chest tombs of Elizabeth Berkeley (d.1596) and her son Thomas (d.1611)*
BELOW: *One of the east windows of the east crypt, which was opened in the 1990s to reveal that the chamber beyond was full of worked stone, though built originally as a burial crypt*

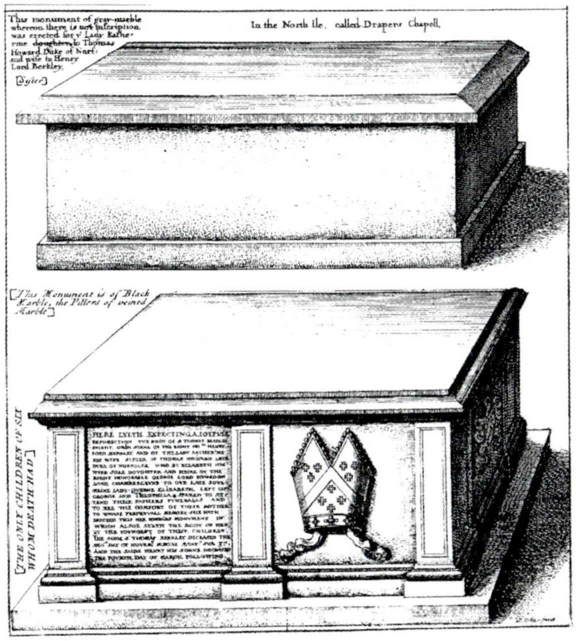

door or windows, access was probably obtained via an internal staircase, which was sealed with a stone slab after each burial.

The seventeenth century

The new religion took firm hold during the long reign of Queen Elizabeth (1558–1603). The interior of St Michael's was inevitably altered, but it is impossible to say whether the major cause of these changes was iconoclasm or gradual deterioration and neglect. In 1608 a thief, pretending that he was acting on official instructions, stole all the brasses from the gravestones and tombs inside the church. During the incumbencies of Presbyterian vicars in the mid-seventeenth century, any vestiges of the old religion were finally eliminated: inscriptions were painted out, the brass eagle was sold, the font taken down and the cross in the Mercers' Chapel removed.

By 1600 the pulpit was replacing the high altar as the focus of attention in the new liturgy. In St Michael's the removal of the rood screen allowed the introduction of a pulpit, and in 1602 it was furnished with a great hourglass to measure the time devoted to the sermon. Box pews were erected for the first time, the richest families paying the highest pew rents to sit closest to the pulpit. The nave of the medieval church is unlikely to have had any seating and would have presented an essentially empty space as far the rood screen. As the nave filled with pews they covered the pavement floor which was 'almost all Tomb-stones, and some very ancient'. The poor were forced farther to the back and very often stood during services. Such was the demand to be close to the front that galleries had to be constructed.

The craft companies maintained their chapels for varying lengths of time. The Drapers paid their last annual rent in 1697, but would appear to have ceased using their chapel well before that date. In 1613 the Mercers completely renovated their chapel, paying their last rent in 1712. In 1628 the Cappers surrendered their chapel, retaining only six seats, and a later arrangement allowed them the use of the room over the south porch. This then became known as the Cappers' Chamber and payments for its repair are recorded as late as 1821. There is no trace of the Smiths' Company using their chapel after 1560. The Girdlers paid an annual rent for both their chapel

A PROSPECT OF SAINT MICHAELS CHURCH IN COVENTRY
This Stately Church but view it well
Inside and out, ther's few excell,
Lofty, Spatious, Spyre so high
It may be said to touch the Sky.
Built of good, firm, & Lasting stone
Carv'd Curiously, and Lively done.
THIS
Church is in lenth from the Northwest corner of the Steeple, to the East end of ye Chancell, 100 yards: But in measuring, Remember, to allow 8, because ye corner of ye Church covers so much of the Steeple. The Height of the Steeple to the first Batlement is 50 yards.
ane half in measuring of which you must allow 2 yards & ane half because ye lower Batlement hids so much of the foot of it. The height of the Spyre is 42 yards of the which you must allow 2 for the forgoing reason.
A Scale of yards
Done by Alexander Forbes anno Dom: 1691

and chamber, this last perhaps constructed as an enclosed gallery. In 1626 the chamber also contained a library but some time thereafter it was vacated and the structure was eventually demolished. The Dyers had abandoned their chapel by 1639.

The withdrawal of most of the craft companies from St Michael's in the seventeenth century released space for other uses. A greater floor area became available for burials and wealthy families would pay handsomely for designated space. By the middle of the century, brick vaults were being leased under the floors of the abandoned craft chapels. The earliest known instance is dated 1659, when a vault beneath the Mourners' Chapel, the former Dyers' Chapel, was let to Mrs Strode, wife of William Strode. In 1690 the Vestry agreed that George Fulwood should have a 'burying place at the upper end of the Girdlers Chappell'. This was probably beneath the easternmost bay of the outer north aisle. In 1703 the vault was taken over by Dorothy Purefoy, his mother-in-law, who in the same year also erected a monument on the east wall of the chapel to her three deceased daughters and her husband. The former Girdlers' Chapel was used by the Consistory Court and was first fitted out for the purpose in 1634. Two early eighteenth-century references confirm this location.

In 1587 the 'Charnel House' (west crypt) was let to persons unknown, possibly as a private burial vault. From this time bones were probably stored in the east crypt, the former chapel of the Trinity Guild. In the 1640s five shillings was paid 'for cleansing the Charnel House & layeing the bones and sculles in order'. The crypt was still being used as a charnel house as late as 1818. The mass of skulls and bones probably blocked the door and staircase that once led up to the chancel. The west crypt continued to be let as family vaults. In 1690 the Vestry agreed that George Bohun (Bowne) should have a sixth part of 'the vault under the North side of the Church' to construct a vault of stone or brick in the south-west corner, paying five shillings a year. In 1701 the bay to the east was let to the Bridgeman family at a similar rate. The process of dividing the crypt began conveniently in the farthest corner from the door.

It does not appear that much attention was paid to the exterior fabric of the church in the 150 years following the Reformation. By the end of the seventeenth century the finer stone detailing was crumbling, particularly the window tracery. In 1690 six windows were repaired or rebuilt, including the 'north' and 'south' windows in the chancel, 'now... very dangerous'. A further seven windows were rebuilt in 1694. In the same year, a programme of repair was also prepared for the steeple. The work was estimated to cost £200, levied, with some resistance, on the parishioners and was completed by the spring of 1696.

The eighteenth century

By the beginning of the eighteenth century, the fabric of the church had deteriorated such that it was 'much out of order in severall parts of it', and levies for its repair were imposed on the parishioners in 1706, 1715 and 1726. Most of the nearly £400 raised was spent on works to the interior.

The erection of more galleries further transformed the appearance of the church interior. The architect Mr Smith of Warwick was employed to design a gallery for the north side of the nave. This was erected around 1725–26 and the work included the demolition of the Girdlers' Chapel in the outer north aisle. At the same time it was also agreed that the gallery on the south side of the church should be enlarged. Another major change was the erection of a gallery at the west end of the church, ordered in November 1730 to support an organ. The organ builder was Thomas Swarbrick of Warwick (1679–1752) who created 'a masterpiece... presumably an organ-harpsichord on a grand scale'.

By 1726 the original staircase rising to the Cappers' Chamber, situated over the south porch, had become unusable. A connection was therefore made to the gallery immediately to the east over the former Cappers' Chapel. Today a blocked door and metal balcony can be seen at high level in the wall between the Cappers' Room and the former Cappers' Chapel. Around 1748 the well-known Warwick mason William Hiorne or Hiorns was employed to make significant alterations to the high altar. The work raised the level of the altar, blocking the existing vestry door on the south side of the apse and requiring a new vestry doorway from the Mercers' Chapel. The vestry on the south-east side of the church was a trapezoidal-shaped two-storey building, known to

OPPOSITE: *The earliest known elevation, strictly speaking a prospect, of St Michael's, made by Alexander Forbes in 1691. He also provides the first measurements of the length of the church and the height of the steeple*

OVERLEAF: *The modern city viewed through the east window of the Drapers' Chapel*

OPPOSITE: *Interior looking west, by William Turner of Allesley, 1839. The organ gallery (early 1730s) can be seen in the distance, obscuring the tower arch, and the medieval decoration of the timber roof is still evident*

RIGHT: *J. Drayton Wyatt's sketch (early 1850s) of the apse and the none-too-elegant vestry extension added below it in the mid eighteenth century, viewed from the former Half Moon Inn rear yard, soon to become St Mary Street*

BELOW RIGHT: *The steps leading from the Mercers' Chapel down into Bayley Lane, thought to be mid-eighteenth century*

have incorporated an earlier timber-framed building. It did not conform in style or plan to the three bays of the fifteenth-century vestry situated on the north and east sides of the apse. The external door from the Mercers' Chapel, with steps leading directly onto Bayley Lane, may also have been made at some time in the mid-eighteenth century.

A view of Hiorns' altarpiece appears in an illustration of about 1800. It was a decidedly classical piece, tripartite in form and occupying the three inner bays of the apse, the centre panel surmounted by a round arch. The two outer bays of the apse were simply plastered, but the whole composition partially obscured all five apsidal windows. Massive rose-coloured swagged curtains completed the incongruous design. The blocking of the apsidal windows can clearly be seen in later paintings of the church exterior.

When the rents for family vaults did not materialise, the Vestry sought others willing to pay. By 1718 the daughter of William Strode, Lady Bedingfeld of

LEFT: *William Hiorn's classical altarpiece of* C. *1748, illustrated in about 1800. The red drapery obscured the lower part of the magnificent apse windows*

BELOW: *Exterior view of St Michael's from the north-east by Edward Rudge, 1823–25, showing the blocking of the apse windows by Hiorn's altarpiece and drapery*

Barston, Warwickshire, was in arrears for the vault in the Dyers'/Mourners' Chapel, first let to her family in 1659. It was not until 1747, however, that an agreement was made with the Inge family of the Charterhouse to take it over.

By the mid-eighteenth century the top of the spire had been repaired a number of times. From 1655 to 1750 there were at least four instances of damage by lightning. In 1730 a gilded copper dragon was made to replace the old weathercock at the top of the steeple, but 'the gilded monster' proved too heavy and was replaced in 1734 by a new weather-cock and a globe, also made in copper. This in turn was taken down in 1743. In 1674 the six bells in the steeple had been cast into eight and a century later, in 1774, the eight bells were recast and two more added, weighing nearly seven tons altogether. One of the earliest views of St Michael's is of the tower at about this time, when the west and south sides were still surrounded by houses. In 1784 most of these building were demolished, the ground taken into the graveyard in June 1786 consecrated for burial.

RIGHT: *View from the north-west by Moses Griffith, 1776, showing buildings still crowded round the base of the tower*

BELOW RIGHT: *The earliest known plan of the church interior, 1790s*

The weight of the new peal of bells and its effect on the stability of the tower caused considerable concern. In July 1794 James Wyatt and Joseph Potter reported on the state of the tower, recommending that the bells be taken down from the belfry and that an internal frame be constructed at ground level in order to bear their weight. The new structure reduced the height of the bells in the tower by 30ft. Decayed and fractured stones were also replaced and the tower reinforced with iron bands set into the stonework. The total cost of the work, completed in December 1794, was well over £2,500

The earliest known plan of the church interior dates from the 1790s. It shows the main walls and piers, but no pews or galleries. The positions of the chapels are marked, varying slightly from traditionally accepted locations.

The nineteenth-century restoration

The nineteenth century saw a proliferation of topographical paintings and architectural drawings of St Michael's. The earliest interior view is a watercolour produced around 1800, taken from the west

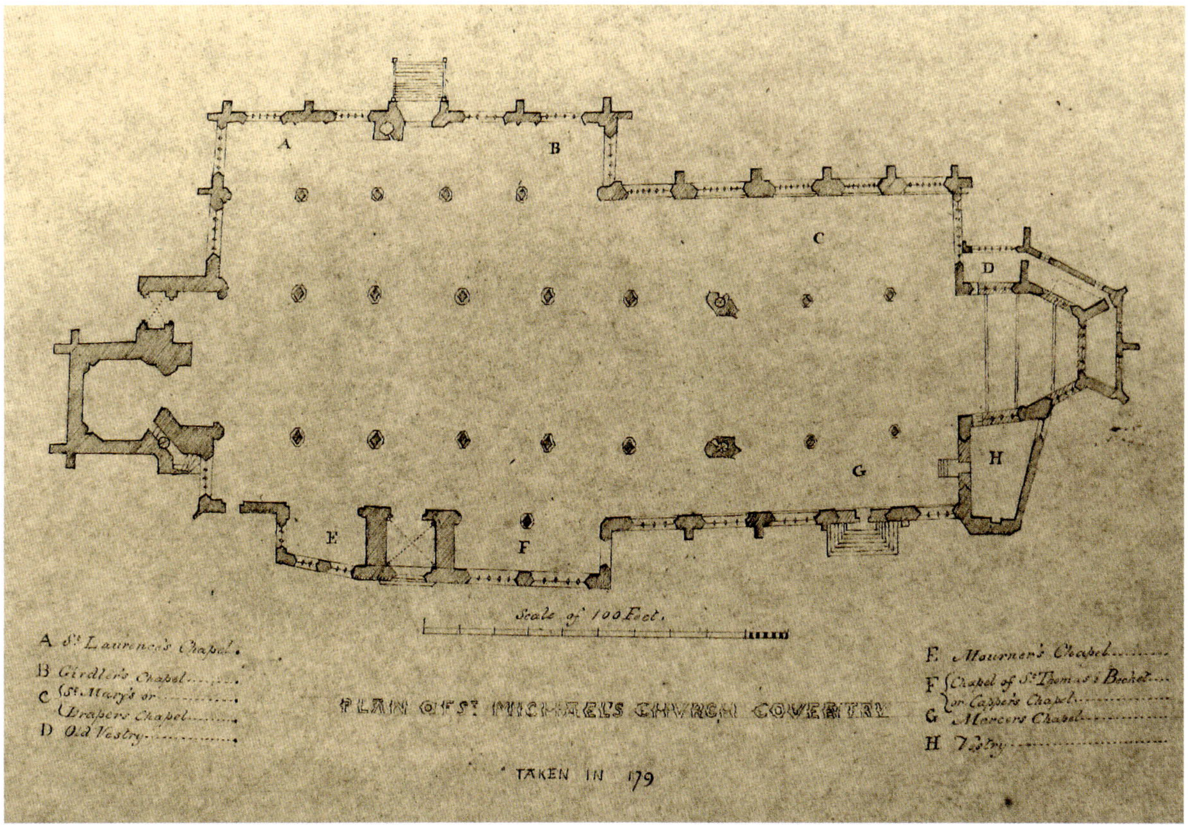

The earliest view of the interior of St Michael's, a watercolour by Henry Jeayes, c.1800. Over two centuries, the church has filled with galleries and box pews, but the west end is decidedly empty of any seating

end, and showing the box pews and the galleries in the north and south aisles as distinctive features. The altarpiece, with its rose-pink curtains, terminates the distant view of the east end. On the left, the former Girdlers' Chapel is empty except for a balustrade, which may have demarcated the area assigned to the Consistory Court. On the right, the wall of the south porch appears to have been plastered and the arch leading through is blocked.

Thomas Sharp, appointed churchwarden in 1794, published the first detailed history of the church in 1818 and the traditional identification of the medieval chapels is derived from his work. In the same year, advice was taken regarding the stability of the spire, and the whole structure was repointed and two of the corner pinnacles of the tower and the top 32ft (9.7m) of the spire rebuilt. The work, costing more than £100, led the Vestry to realise that the rebuilding and restoring of the church could no longer be sustained by the parish rate and that subscriptions should be sought from the city and neighbourhood.

> The Parishioners of St Michaels trust that their beautiful Spire so ornamental to the surrounding countryside may be considered as a national object and that the present appeal to the public will not be made in vain.

It is interesting that as early as 1818 St Michael's was regarded as a national monument, which it was appropriate to maintain from sources beyond the parish.

In 1830 William Reader, an antiquarian, and churchwarden from 1821 to 1823, listed the vaults and many of the burial slabs that made up much of the floor. It is fortunate that he made his record before the great change to the interior of some 20 years later. The west crypt, described as a charnel house, still contained two vaults, one holding around ten coffins belonging to the Bohun family and the other two coffins belonging to the Bridgeman family. The Strode vault under the former Dyers' Chapel on the south side contained seven family coffins with one belonging to the Inge family. The majority of the burial slabs Reader recorded dated from the eighteenth century and it is probable that the inscriptions on most of the earlier stones had become illegible or had been entirely worn away. It is also very likely that earlier burials had been replaced by more recent ones, as space in the crowded church floor was at a premium.

As the century progressed, architectural taste moved away from the classical style towards a growing appreciation of medieval Gothic. The great Coventry antiquarian, Benjamin Poole, writing in 1870, subjected the earlier work in the church to scathing criticism:

> It must be told, however, that up to nearly the close of the first half of the present century this scene was greatly obscured and damaged by the absurd and anomalous accumulation of pews, galleries, and staircases; such a wild spread and pile of incumbrances certainly as no other church could have found room for.

As early as 1803 a generous legacy of £1,000 was left to re-pew the church. In 1820 Stedman Thomas Whitwell was appointed to prepare plans, which swept away everything in the interior, except for the organ, to provide 'kneelings' for 2,700 people. A plan, dated 1818 and possibly by Whitwell, is the earliest measured drawing of the church and shows the disposition of the existing pews and other fittings. In the event, it was not until 1844 that the Vestry finally decided to remove the 'ill-adapted' pews and galleries. The new pews were to include both appropriated (fee-paying) and free, and in late 1845 Messrs Scott and Moffat of London were appointed as designers. Although the 1803 legacy had grown to over £2,000, additional funding and grants were needed to meet the estimated cost of £2,950. The 1845 Scott and Moffat plan contains useful information on other internal arrangements in the church.

The stripping out of the church began in the spring of 1849, when a uniform scheme of low oak 'seats' was installed. The pulpit was moved from the stair pier on the north side of the church to that on the south. The organ was placed on a low platform at the extreme west end, the high original gallery having been removed. An intriguing watercolour, seemingly painted after the stripping out and before the re-pewing, shows an entirely empty church. There is no sign of the Hiorns' altarpiece, although a series of gravestones surviving in the floor at the west end is clearly visible.

In 1851 work moved directly on to removing the 'coatings of paint and divers coloured washings' that

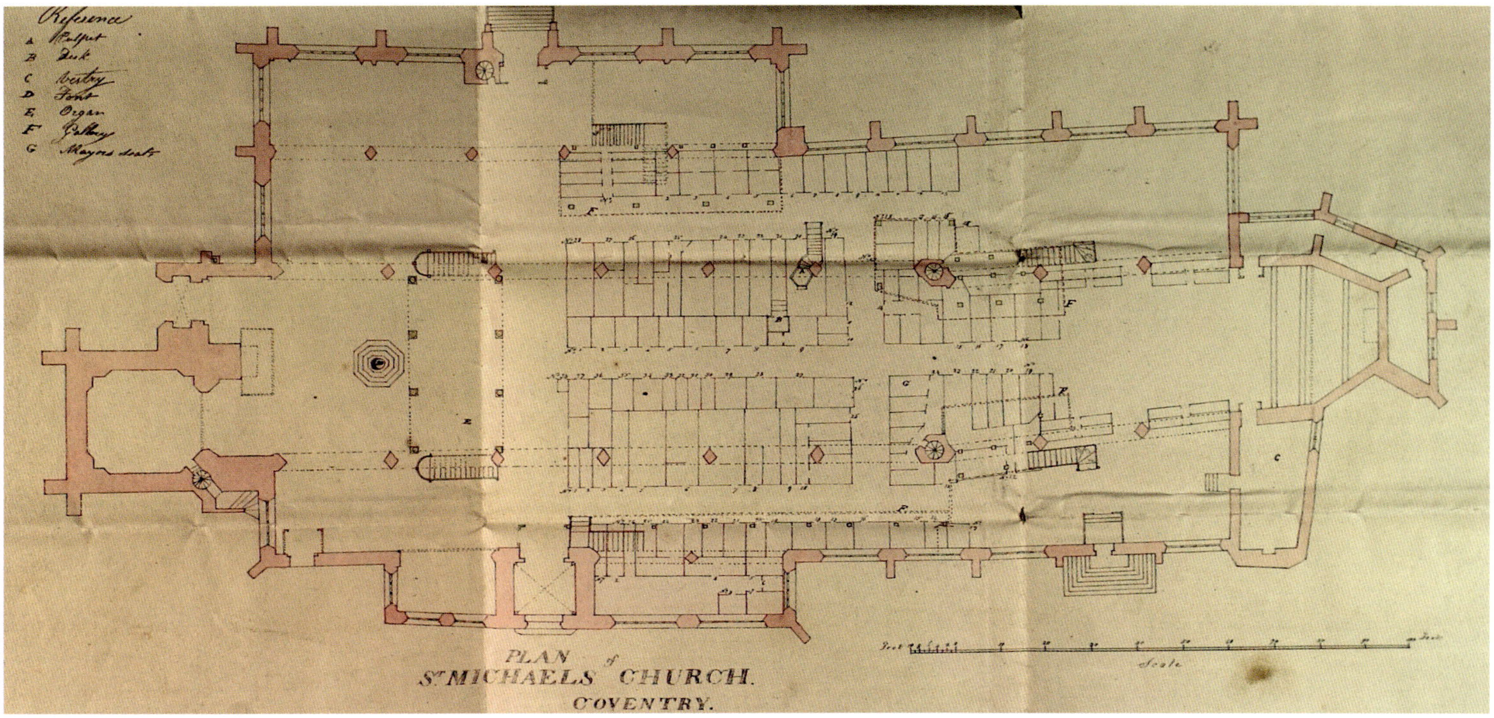

Plan of St Michael's in 1817, possibly by Stedman Thomas Whitwell. This is the earliest known measured drawing showing the galleries and pews and confirms the emptiness of the church at the west end, except for the organ gallery and font

had accumulated over the centuries on the stone surfaces of the interior. It is probable that every layer, including any medieval decorative scheme, was removed down to the bare stone. Benjamin Poole questioned the justification of the:

> extensive pulling down and removal of monuments and tombstones, and changing their places to entirely different parts of the church; ... some memorial stones may have been entirely lost in the process.

Much of this work would now be regarded as unnecessarily destructive of fabric and a great loss to the history of the church. The new taste, disapproving strongly of the classical altarpiece, sought a high-minded harmony with the Gothic architecture of the building.

The stripping out of the old seating also provided the opportunity of 'tidying up' the floor of the church. In 1849 the floor of the Drapers' Chapel, composed of flat gravestones, was covered with a foot of soil and a new tile floor laid on top. The same happened in the chancel, covering or removing the grave slabs that can clearly be seen in a view taken about ten years before (see p.60,). More drastic action took place in the west and east crypts:

> ...the vaults or 'bone-houses,' as they were called...were thoroughly cleared out, and the immense accumulation of human bones, of which these vaults during a vast number of years had become a receptacle, were quietly removed and buried during the night.

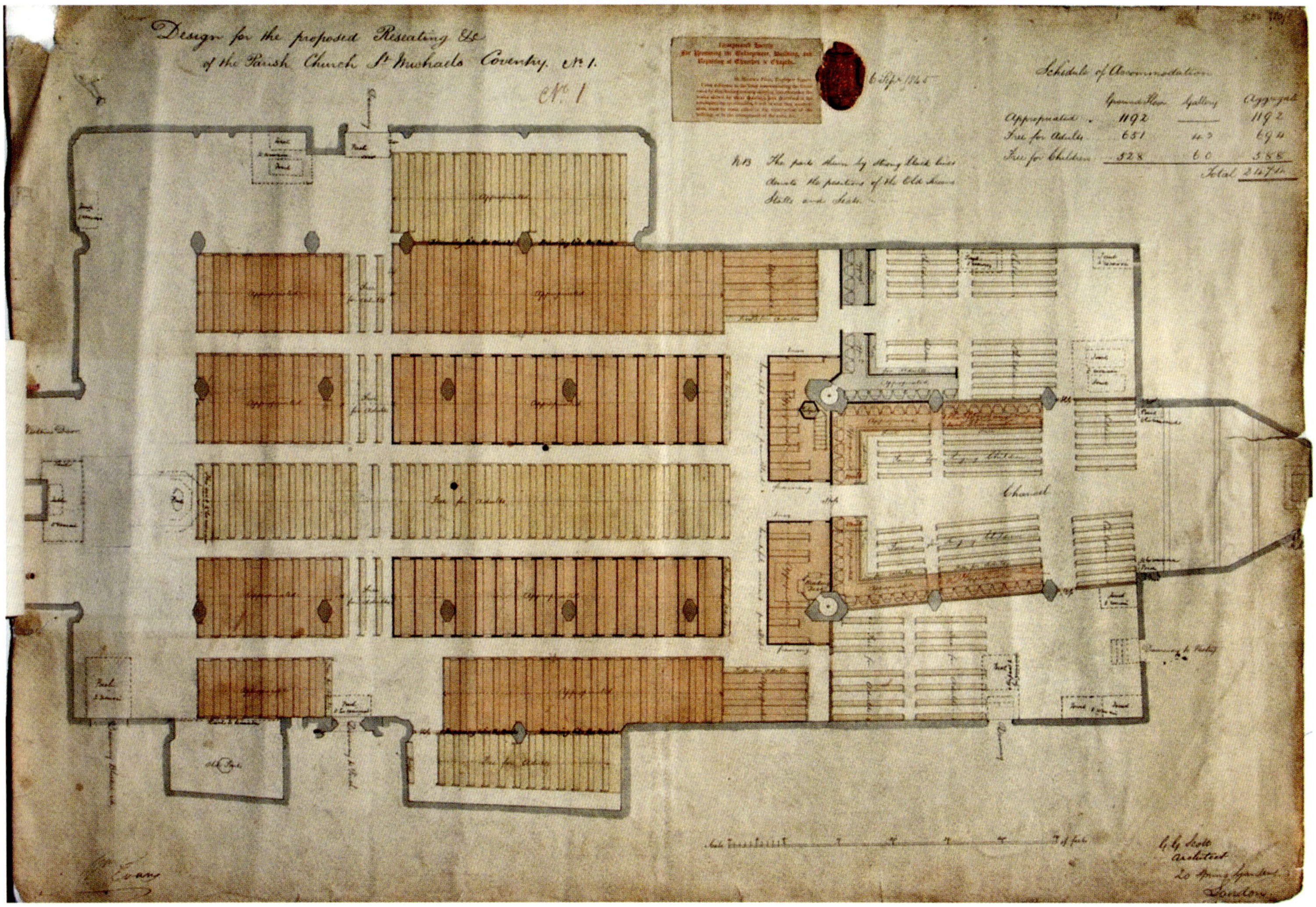

Plan drawn up by the architects Scott and Moffat in 1845 for the reordering of the interior, introducing seating of 'uniform use and shape'. The new pews, including free sittings, would now stretch farther back as a result of the removal of the organ gallery

It is likely that the staircase that led up into the church from the east vault was discovered on removing the bones, but it was not opened up until after 1870.

In 1860 a new ornate Gothic altarpiece designed by James Murray, a local architect, replaced the eighteenth-century classical version. He introduced new blind arcading below the windows in the four outer bays of the apse, with a more elaborate reredos occupying the centre bay. In removing the classical altarpiece, fragments of the original medieval scheme were revealed, including the vestry door. Hiorns' corniced and panelled door, installed in 1749, can be seen in a view from the apse, dated 1839 (see p.60). Above this door, a large classical monument blocks the lowest tier of the apse window. This was also removed in Murray's scheme.

By the mid-nineteenth century the increasing deterioration of the church fabric could no longer be ignored. Plans for the restoration of the exterior of St Michael's began in 1851, when the architect George Gilbert Scott reported on the state of the tower and spire. The stone vault at the top of the tower had been removed for the bell frame constructed in 1794 and the great arch into the nave had been blocked

ABOVE: *An eerily empty view of the interior looking east by Nathaniel Troughton, c.1850, executed soon after the stripping out of the old galleries and box pews. This confirms that the medieval glass had survived in the clerestoreys*
RIGHT: *This photograph, possibly from the 1930s, shows James Murray's altarpiece of c.1860, which once again allowed all the apse windows to be revealed after a century in which the lower parts were blocked. Medieval glass had been arranged in the two outer windows, and new glass placed in the centre three*

up, leaving only a small doorway. Although the frame was meant to be free-standing, Scott discovered that it was using the tower for support and recommended that bell-ringing should cease. The solution was to restore the tower to its original form, with either a strongly framed new floor to carry the bells or a separate campanile in the churchyard. The bells were not rung for two years until, in 1853, Mr Wyatt, 'a surveyor and architect of high repute', reported that the tower was not in any danger. Bell-ringing was then resumed.

John Drayton Wyatt was George Gilbert Scott's assistant, and 34 of his sketch perspectives, elevations and details, all made around 1852, have survived. These must belong to the preliminary survey work, since by March 1853 Gilbert Scott had started work on the restoration of the exterior stonework. Wyatt produced splendid watercolour elevations and cross-sections which constitute the first measured drawings of the north and south elevations. These represent the church as it was intended to look after the repair of the stonework and no major modifications were planned, at least on the north elevation, to the size, shape, and disposition of the windows, or to their tracery. On the south elevation, however, it was intended to block the present doorway to the west of the former Dyers' Chapel and to extend the vestry around the south and east side of the apse, a project not completed until 1886–87. Otherwise the windows were to be restored as found. There was certainly some regard shown for historical detail, since the vertical joint on the exterior of south aisle, still visible today, was marked with the note 'straight joint to be preserved' (see p.35).

Work on replacing the outer face of the stonework began in 1854 with the south side of the church. A series of new crocketted pinnacles was placed on all the aisle parapets; judging from earlier views these had clearly been missing for some time. The

ABOVE: *A watercolour of the north vestry door and north window in the apse by Nathaniel Troughton, c.1850. This was the state of the apse after the classical altar piece was removed, revealing mutilated medieval painted decoration and stone mouldings*

LEFT: *The westernmost window of the outer north aisle, drawing by Nathaniel Troughton, 18 August 1859, demonstrating the drastic restoration of the exterior stonework and windows*

re-facing was a prolonged affair, owing to the expensive and laborious nature of the work. An important sketch of the westernmost bay of the outer north aisle under repair, dated 22 August 1859, shows the whole of the exterior stripped of its ashlar face and the parapet entirely demolished, exposing the roof joists. All of the tracery and its flanking interior blind arches were also removed so that the two-centred interior arch became visible on the exterior. This view of the work, if it is typical of the campaign, confirms that the restoration involved the complete renewal of major areas of exterior stonework, including window tracery. The simple late-fifteenth-century five-light tracery of the outer aisle north windows was intended to be preserved, but in the end the tracery was rebuilt in a more elaborate pattern, as can be seen today. This change was associated with the installation of new memorial windows. Work continued gradually until 1870, with the west porch restored in that year, re-opening a doorway blocked for many years. The tower, the clerestory elevations, the apse and the vestry remained in a state of dilapidation until the 1885–90 restoration.

The exterior fabric not so far repaired, continued to deteriorate; in 1869 George Gilbert Scott again reported on the state of the tower, recommending immediate action. He eloquently described its 'melancholy dilapidation':

The westernmost window of the north aisle, shown under restoration in Troughton's sketch opposite, is seen here with its new and more intricate pattern of tracery

> Its exterior is, in fact a mere wreck, crumbling constantly away, the dust of disintegration falling in heaps about its base, and masses of stone from time to time falling down, making increased destruction of the parts which they strike in their passage, and endangering the passers by... The beautiful groups of pinnacles and buttresses are only kept together by irons and cement, being shattered in a thousand pieces....

Scott estimated the costs of repair would be in the region of £16,000.

A section at the summit of the spire had in fact been rebuilt in 1861 following a fall of stone, one piece of which had broken through the roof and landed on the floor near the organ. This undertaking was daringly accomplished without scaffolding by the builder, Mr Frith. He clambered out of the top light in the spire and, by a system of ropes, pulleys and a platform, managed to ascend to the top and bring down the weathercock and globe to the ground for refurbishment and re-gilding.

Sometime before 1870, the monument to Dame Mary Bridgeman, wife of Orlando Bridgeman, originally situated on the south side of the chancel, was moved to the east wall of the Dyers' Chapel, where it still stands today. Both husband and wife

The north side of St Michael's and its cemetery; a painting in primitive style by J.D. Walker, 1810, showing clearly the hummocky nature of the cemetery after centuries of burials in a space inadequate to cope with the expanding population of the parish

had been buried on the opposite side of the church, however, in the west crypt. A detailed survey of the monuments was published in 1884 with a plan. This remains the only reliable way of identifying the shattered and mostly illegible survivals of the Blitz, unless they were subsequently moved. It also meticulously describes each of the memorial windows that had been installed in the decades previously. They were all destroyed in the Blitz, as none were removed before hostilities to a safer place; until recently it was thought that some of these Victorian windows had found their way during the war to two churches in Iceland.

Fortunately the 1884 survey was published before the second large-scale restoration of the church, which began in 1885. Most of the information on this scheme is derived from volumes of newspaper cuttings compiled by Alderman William Andrews, who was an active and informed member of the Restoration Committee. He wrote many of the newspaper articles himself, providing a remarkably detailed account.

In March 1882 a report by James Marriott on the church fabric was presented to the Vestry. The author remarked on the dangerous condition of a truss in the chancel roof and the decayed stonework in the apse, chancel and vestries which, except for the tracery of the windows, required 'complete restoration'. The nave roof and its lead covering were in a better state than that farther east. Only four of the original principal trusses remained, the others having been strengthened with additional timbers which projected upwards through the lead. The cost of the extensive repair work was estimated at £27,000.

It was resolved to consult with the representatives of the late Sir George Gilbert Scott and to seek

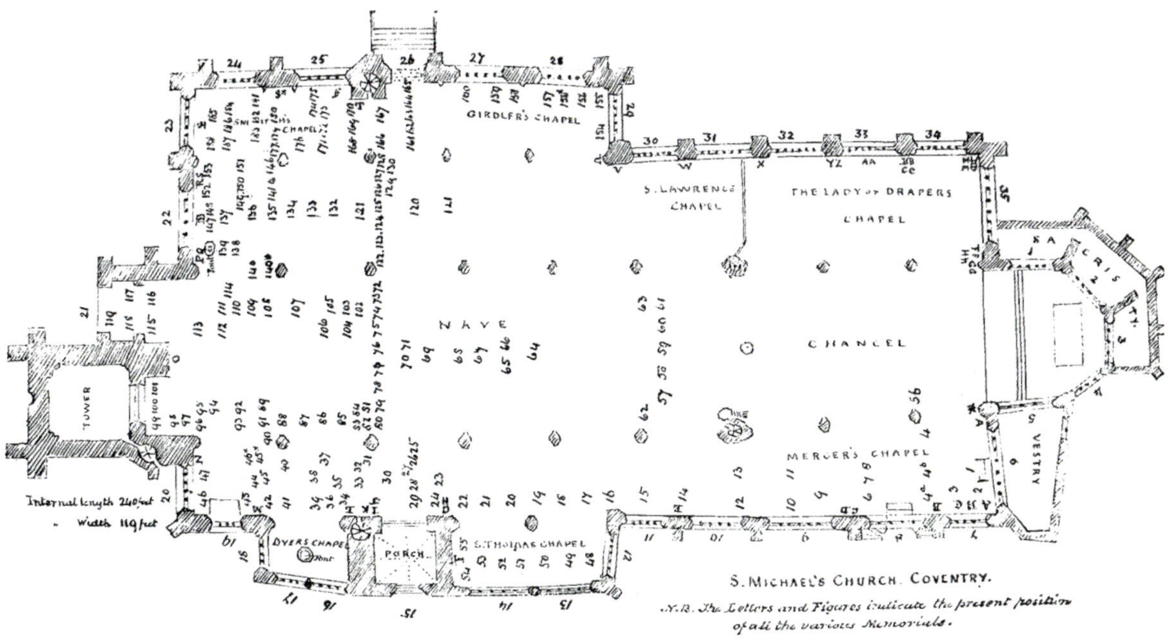

ABOVE: Monument to Dame Mary Bridgeman (d.1701), on the east wall of the Dyers' Chapel; the Bridgemans were buried in the west crypt

RIGHT: A plan of St Michaels by John Astley, 1884, showing the position of wall monuments and of grave slab inscriptions in the floor

funding by public subscription. In June 1882 Scott's son, John Oldrid Scott, submitted a detailed report outlining the repair work needed: an almost complete replacement of the exterior stone face of the apse, chancel, nave and vestry. The exterior tracery and surrounds of the chancel and apse windows had been rendered in cement, smothering any detail. An early photograph confirms the poor condition of the apse windows. The estimate of the repair costs for the body of the church was £12,600, plus another £18,000 for the tower and spire; this had increased by another £4,600 by the time the work was started.

A public meeting was held in St Mary's Guildhall on 26 June 1884. George Woodcock, a wealthy solicitor, businessman and churchwarden of St Michael's, had already offered £10,000, on condition that £20,000 was raised within the year and that the work would be speedily and thoroughly carried out, and £9,500 of the balance was raised at the meeting. A Restoration Committee was appointed and the remainder of the year was spent seeking further subscriptions. By the end of December £20,243 16s 11d had been raised and the vicar, the Rev. James Buller, was able to announce the success of the funding campaign in his Christmas sermon. On 19 January 1885 Oldrid Scott was formally appointed as project architect and in early March he presented his scheme of restoration. Significantly, Scott's proposals did not include re-hanging the bells in the tower, and he suggested that a separate belltower be erected of at least 100ft (30m) in height. This immediately provoked a great deal of discussion and the argument raged for many years. John Thompson, a contractor based in Peterborough, tendered a price of £31,853, but other additional costs were identified, such as removing the bells and taking down the organ. Hardwearing Runcorn stone from Cheshire was selected as the most suitable material for the repairs. Thompson's tender was accepted and work began on site on 2 June 1885, with the north aisle partitioned off so that services could continue. By 9 September the scaffolding was complete, allowing a close examination of the tower and revealing that it was in a more alarming condition than previously thought. The parlous state of the interior was evident after the removal of the 1794 bell frame.

FAR LEFT: *A photo taken from the roof of Holy Trinity before the 1885–90 restoration, showing the extreme dilapidation of the tower and spire and the reinforcing beams inserted into the roof*

LEFT: *A photo of the apsidal end of St Michael's, taken before the exterior was restored in the 1860s*

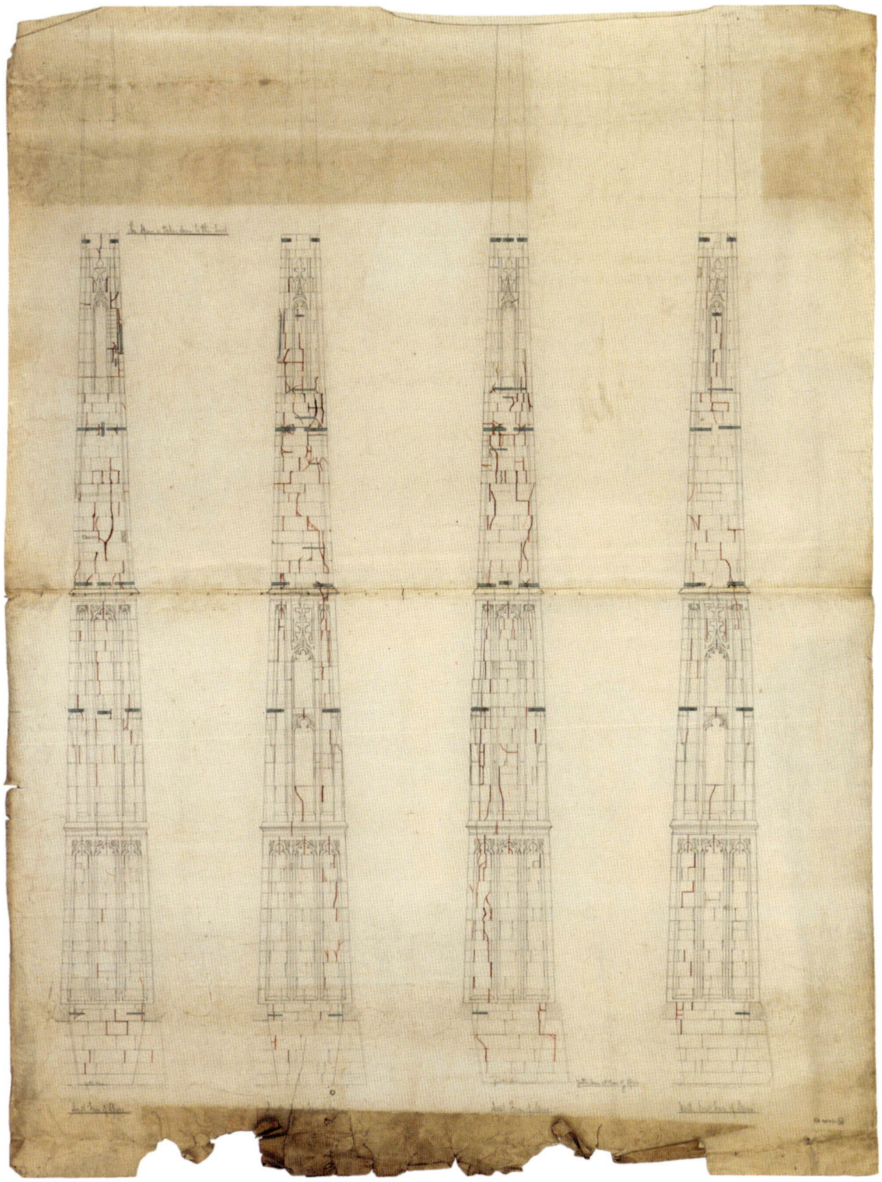

ABOVE: *Drawings for the restoration of the four sides of the spire by John Oldrid Scott, early 1885; the cracks in the fabric are coloured an ominous red and the restraining straps are shown in grey*
RIGHT: *The east arch into the tower was revealed again in the 1885–90 restoration after having been completely blocked, except for a door*

During the foundation investigations in September 1885, it was discovered that the bedrock between 11 and 14½ ft (3.3–4.4m) below the surface of much of the tower abruptly vanished in a vertical face at the north-west corner. A test pit was dug here to a depth of 22ft (6.7m), revealing that the ground was entirely made-up. Cracks immediately began to appear and emergency propping was installed to support the tower so that it could be safely underpinned, work costing £1000, which had not been anticipated. The drop in the bedrock was thought to be a former quarry face, but it is possible that it marks the line of the medieval castle ditch (see p.21). Tests also found that the spire at the weathercock leaned about 34½ ins (870mm) north-west from the perpendicular. In order to reduce the weight of the tower, the top 54ft (16.4m) of the spire was taken down. The dismantling of the bell frame revealed the shattered nature of the interior stonework of the tower and it was decided that both the exterior and interior stonework would need to be refaced. This was carried out to an average depth of about 1ft (30cm). As work proceeded up the tower, the architectural detail of the windows, cornices and niches was all renewed, 'the original details having been exactly reproduced by copying from the most perfect parts of the ancient features that remained'. The groined vault above the third stage of the tower was restored to a design by Oldrid Scott. His many large-scale drawings for the restoration of the tower and spire vividly demonstrate the appalling condition of the stonework, the many cracks coloured an ominous red, held together by a number of horizontal metal straps, probably installed in 1794. Before the restoration, the windows of the lowest three stages

OPPOSITE: *The new statuary and facing stone of the tower, 1886–88*
BELOW: *The tower and spire enveloped in scaffolding, 1886–88*

of the tower had been blocked with stonework. With the arch into the nave also filled with brickwork, the space was used as a store for the coal used in the heating boilers installed by this time and was jokingly referred to as 'the tallest coal hole in England'.

The Runcorn stone purchased for the scheme arrived in Coventry from Cheshire by canal and the main masons' workshop was established at the basin. A 25hp portable engine was positioned on the canal bank to run the saws which converted the rough stone into ashlar blocks. The finished stone was then carted to the church.

Not surprisingly, the restoration of the decrepit tower and spire gained more attention than the other repairs to the church. The change in the appearance of the tower was particularly visible and dramatic, as eroded and crumbling stonework and featureless statuary were replaced with crisp stone detail and 40 newly sculpted statues. The work to the body of the church included a major overhaul and repairs to the roof, the decoration of the chancel ceiling, the renewal of the external walls of the apse, cleaning and re-insertion of the painted glass windows, provision of a new vestry on the south side of the apse, the re-facing of the clerestory and the tracery of 24 windows, the cleaning of the internal walls and the erection of a new organ. Many of the roof tie beams had failed, some in two or three places. Fifty trusses in all were cut down the centre and wrought iron flitch plates were inserted and bolted through at intervals of 2–3ft (600–900mm). The metal plates proved catastrophic on the night of 14 November 1940, as they twisted in the heat and helped bring the roof down.

The massive restoration project lasted nearly five years and was completed in April 1890. No plans for the remainder of the church survive, except for the scheme to finish the vestry encirclement of the apse on the south side. In April 1886 John Oldrid Scott received approval to spend £1,483. During the demolition of the old trapezoidal vestry some foundations were uncovered, confirming the once close proximity of buildings to the church.

By Easter 1887 the first phase of work had been completed on the body of the church, and the nave and south aisle were opened for worship at a ceremony led by the bishop of Worcester. A new organ by Henry Willis and Son of London was installed in the south chancel aisle in time for the occasion. Attention then turned to the north aisles, where more wrought iron flitch plates were inserted into the roof trusses. The facing work on the tower had started in February 1886 and the spire was finally topped on 1 August 1888. The restoration ended with a grand opening ceremony on 22 April 1890.

In July 1891 the contactor, Thompsons, was still owed nearly £6,000 out of a total sum of £39,014. The deficit was mostly covered by a promise of a further £500 from George Woodcock and a mortgage of £4,500 on the church estate. Unfortunately a major dispute then broke out over the payment of the vicar's rate, which delayed the final settlement for a number of years. In June 1895 a Grand Bazaar

Drawing of the separate campanile by John Oldrid Scott, 1886; this was proposed as a possible solution to the controversy over the re-hanging of the bells

RIGHT: *St Michael's after the restoration of 1885–90. Note the smoothness of the roof plane; metal flitch plates had been inserted into the beams under the lead and the projecting reinforcing beams removed*

FAR RIGHT: *John Oldrid Scott's plan for the extension to the vestry, c.1886, the circuit of the apse finally completed after nearly four centuries*

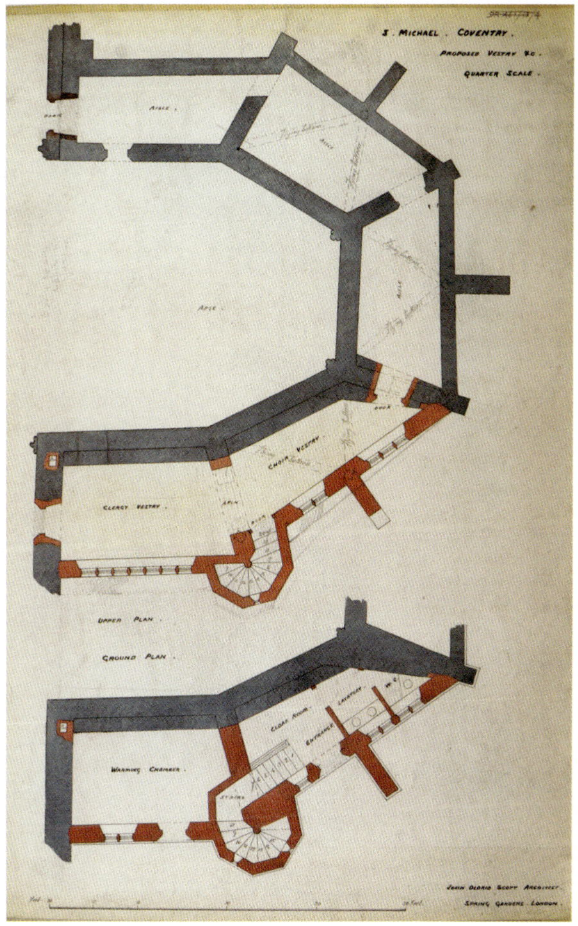

managed to raise over £1,000, which was sufficient not only to pay off the contractors but also to hang the bells.

From the beginning of the project, the future location of the ten bells occupied many hours of discussion and argument. One view held that the bells should be re-hung in the tower to ring a full peal as before; subscriptions for the restoration had in fact been received with this purpose in mind. Oldrid Scott was vehemently opposed to their re-hanging, particularly from the structural point of view; the tower would need to be radically altered to create a suitably sturdy ringing chamber. The complete demolition and replacement of the tower was even suggested, but the solution proposed for the interim was a separate campanile in the churchyard for which Oldrid Scott provided a design. George Woodcock was willing to pay for half of its cost and was a leading proponent of the scheme.

A suggested compromise was to re-install the bells but only allow them to chime. Public opinion was in favour of the re-instatement of a full peal but was also aware of the danger this could cause to the stability of the newly restored tower. There was also general opposition to the radical alterations in the structure and appearance of the newly restored tower which would be needed to allow the bells to peal. In March 1891 the architects, Paley and Austin of Lancaster, produced another design for a campanile, but with Woodcock's death in May 1891 the scheme was quickly abandoned.

The ten bells were finally re-hung in the tower in September 1895. They were installed in the octagon 50ft (15.2m) above the newly restored vault. Messrs Taylor of Loughborough carried out the work under the supervision of John Oldrid Scott, and Messrs Potts and Sons of Leeds replaced the clock and chimes. The bells, which could only be used to chime, were hung in three rows off steel girders let into the stonework.

By 1890 the church had been entirely renewed at a cost of roughly £3.3m in today's terms. As a result very little, if any, of the medieval fabric was visible on the exterior, including the tracery of the windows. Only the interior walls and piers appear to have survived from the medieval period relatively unscathed, but even here any contemporary or later painting or wall washes had been stripped off in the mid-nineteenth century. It is impossible to judge the quantity of medieval timberwork in the roof that had survived the restoration, or to estimate how much remained of the ancient pavement of gravestones which had once covered the floor. The area had been much reduced in size by the introduction of fashionable encaustic tile flooring.

Before the 1885–90 restoration, the coffins in the Strode/Inge vault under the former Dyers' Chapel were removed and the vault closed up. The lead coffins in the west crypt belonging to the Bohun family were still in place in their corner vault, numbering thirteen adults and four children. The fate of the Bridgeman coffins in the next vault is unknown. An anonymous memoir dating from around 1885 to some years after 1922 states 'that within living memory [the west crypt] contained a number of lead coffins'. It would appear that these were removed, perhaps during the restoration, for in 1909 the crypt 'contained fragments that have been removed or discovered in the course of various restorations'. These included a number of decayed statues from the tower, perhaps the best preserved medieval examples.

Around the turn of the twentieth century the noteworthy discovery was made of a previously

The first known measured plan of the west crypt, by John Drayton Wyatt, early 1860s. The use of this crypt as a private burial vault ceased in the late nineteenth century and the coffins were removed

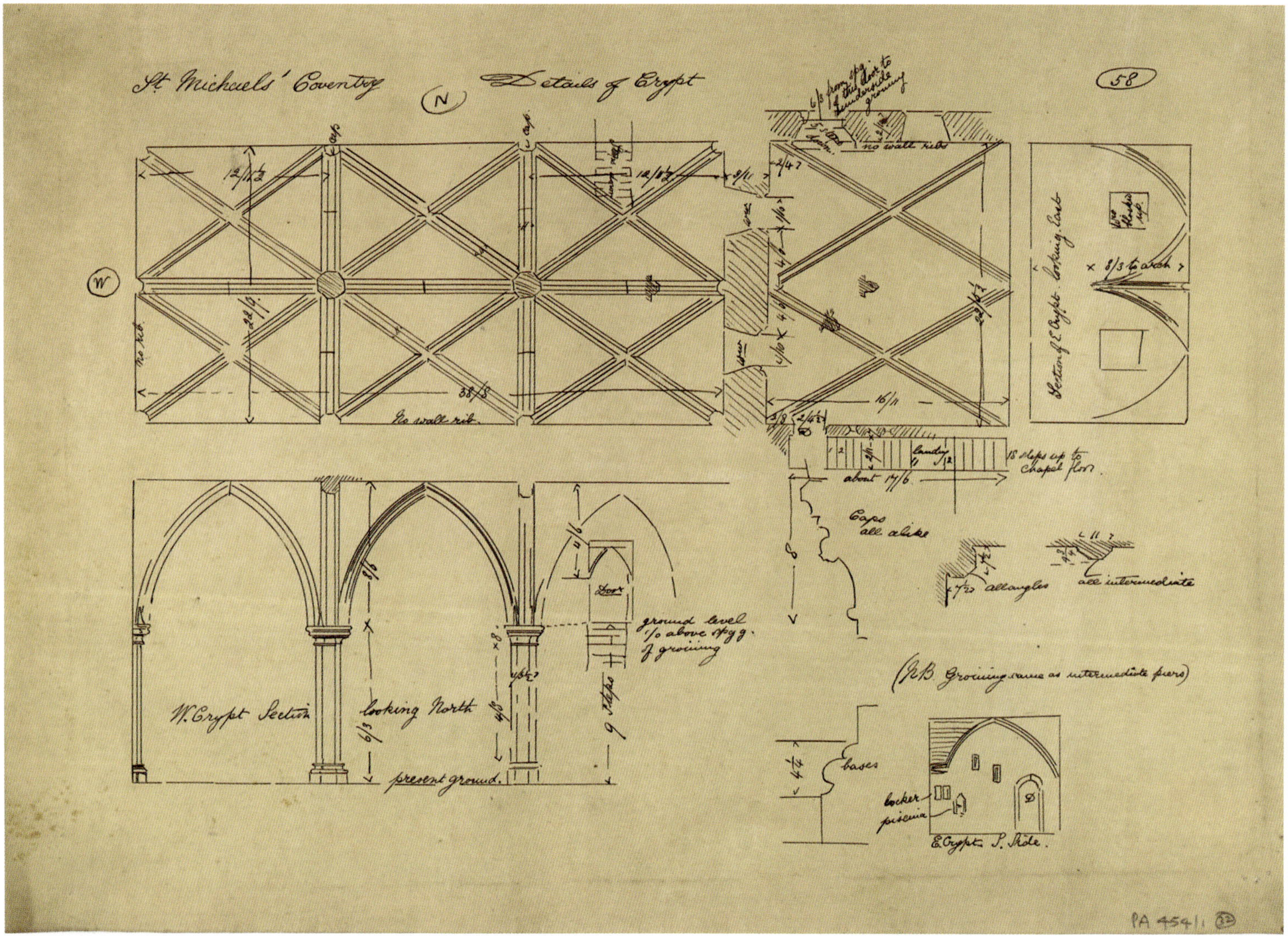

Effigy of H.W. Yeatman-Biggs, appointed Coventry's first post-Reformation bishop in 1918

unknown vault under the former Drapers'/Lady Chapel, when a memorial stone was being laid in the floor and part of it collapsed. The verger, John Owen, was summoned and 'lowered a candle through the hole, and saw coffins ranged on shelves all round a capacious vault'. The location is close to the present position of the Bishop Yeatman-Biggs effigy and is perhaps the vault now full of stone next to the east crypt (see p.55). It may contain the coffins of the Berkeley family, placed there around the turn of the seventeenth century, and had no broken stone within it when investigated during the 1895–90 restoration. At that time, two windows in the east wall of the east crypt were opened in search of further crypts but 'None were discovered, only brick vaults containing lead coffins…'

St Michael's becomes a cathedral, 1900–39

In 1836 the archdeaconry of Coventry, which then formed the southern part of the diocese of Lichfield, was transferred to Worcester. In 1908 the bishop of Worcester, H.W. Yeatman-Biggs, constituted St Michael's as a collegiate church, the first step in making Coventry a separate diocese. World War I interrupted the process, but in 1918 the bishopric of Coventry was formally created and St Michael's church was elevated to cathedral status; Yeatman-Biggs became Coventry's first post-Reformation bishop.

The new cathedral was certainly worthy of its name. It was one of the largest parish churches in the country and had recently been magnificently and expensively restored, with a spire that could compete in height and architectural grandeur with most ancient cathedrals.

Understandably, in the aftermath of such substantial work, no significant changes to St Michael's are recorded in the 40 years from 1900. Canon Atkinson, who retired in 1907, caused the west crypt to be cleared of the rubbish which filled it and be prepared for use as a chapel. The best preserved of the medieval statues, that of St Michael, was placed in the corner of the former Mercers' Chapel but was destroyed in the Blitz. The state and use of the adjoining east crypt at this time is unknown. In 1932, however, the crypt was restored by Sir William Wyley as a memorial chapel for his wife. Sir William was a former mayor of Coventry and for many years senior churchwarden at St Michael's. He died in 1940 and his ashes and those of his wife were interred in the chapel.

Controversy over the bells began again in the mid-1920s, when it was proposed to recast the ten existing bells into a new carillon of fourteen. Strong objections were raised on the grounds of the antiquity of the bells and the fact that, although now only used as a chime, they were capable of ringing a full peal. The dispute culminated in a Consistory Court case in January 1926, now notorious in bell-ringing circles. The attempt to save 'the finest peal of ten bells in the country' from a 'fiery ordeal' failed and the bells were taken down in March 1926 and conveyed to the foundry of Gillett and Johnston in Croydon, where they were recast. The fourteen new bells, with a total weight of over eight tons, were hung in the tower octagon.

In 1935 proposals for altering the sanctuary in the apse were developed by the cathedral architect, W.H. Randall Blacking of Salisbury. These included removing all of James Murray's work of 1860, re-facing the exposed walls, altering the levels of the sanctuary floor and heightening and lengthening the altar. The work was carried out during September and October 1936 by Robert Bridgeman of Lichfield. During the removal of the Victorian floor and arcading, it was discovered that there were at least three, possibly four, earlier floors. The remains of a sedilia were found on the south side, a squint and the ancient door into the vestry on the north side.

The project was a reflection of a growing reaction, under the influence of the modern movement, to the exuberant decoration of the Victorian Gothic period. This encouraged the perception that the 'whole effect of the recent sanctuary was one of restless fussiness'. In the process of restoring 'quiet proportion and harmony' not all was swept away. In fact the approach was archaeologically sensitive, for the newly discovered sedilia, the squint and the door were left as features in the new plain ashlar face and the whole apse was then limewashed. A later commentator reacted in turn to this change in taste by deploring the loss of Murray's design, 'the walls levelled, whitened, and grimly sanitized, the harmonious decorative richness turned to banality'. Blacking's backdrop to the present altar and its charred cross is what is seen by the visitor today, although the coat of limewash has been lost.

The sanctuary following restoration in 1937, when James Murray's elaborate Gothic altarpiece of c.1860 was removed and the walls were limewashed

In October 1938 W.H. Randall Blacking produced a detailed report on the condition of the cathedral church. He was pleased to state that 'with...exceptions the general condition of the fabric is good'. He emphasised that 'little of the original stone facework remains, and we now see, externally, what amounts to a modern refacing of the building...' Structurally, the tower and spire appeared 'to be perfectly sound', as did the bells and their cage. In summary, two years before that fateful day in November 1940, the cathedral was presented as a sound building requiring no major work in the foreseeable future.

5. From destruction to world monument

Only the Victorian glass was left in the cathedral, almost all to be destroyed in November 1940; a few sections survive high up in small trefoils and quatrefoils

The Second World War

One of the first precautionary measures carried out after the outbreak of war on 3 September 1939 was the removal of the medieval glass in the nave clerestory and the two outermost apse windows, the only glass of this period surviving in the cathedral. The process of removal and storage in the cellars of Hampton Lucy Rectory, Warwickshire took several months to complete and cost £600. All the other plain and painted glass, installed mostly during the Victorian period in the aisle window and three innermost windows of the apse, was left *in situ* and was almost completely destroyed in the Blitz.

On the night of 14 October 1940 an incendiary bomb landed on the roof of the cathedral, melting the lead and starting a fire, which was extinguished. This provided a salutary warning, if any were needed, of the vulnerability of this great building in the centre of industrial Coventry. There is no room here to recount in detail the tragic events of the night of 14 November 1940, so eloquently and poignantly described in Provost Howard's *Ruined and Rebuilt*. Only four firewatchers, including the provost, were available that night to protect St Michael's. The primary cause of the destruction was three groups of incendiaries that landed on the extensive low-pitched roofs of the cathedral. As the four men retired exhausted, beaten back by rapidly expanding fires, they expected to lose the whole roof of the building and the furnishings below, but not the walls. Around midnight however, to their horror, the walls of the nave and chancel began to fall to the ground as the intense heat weakened the slender piers. The clerestory and arcade fell too, brought down by the collapse of the roofs as the wrought iron flitch plates, inserted in the trusses during the restoration of the 1880s,

twisted and buckled. By 1.30am the destruction was complete, the fire even taking hold of the vestries via the door from the former Mercers' Chapel. Not only was a substantial part of the cathedral reduced to a pile of smoking rubble, but almost all of the fittings, including the fine medieval misericords in the Lady/Drapers' Chapel, were destroyed. Some small items of value, such as plate, crucifixes, candlesticks and chalices were rescued, however, and the parish registers from 1820 onwards were fortunately saved, but the furniture and vestments in the vestries were reduced to ashes.

The west crypt was being used as an air raid shelter at the time of the raid. Around midnight the occupants were alarmed to hear masonry falling above their heads. They were evacuated to other shelters, but fortunately both east and west crypts with their stone vaulted roofs survived intact. Until the electricity was cut off, the bells in the tower chimed the hours, falsely reassuring many Coventrians that all was well at the cathedral.

The scene that confronted Provost Howard in the morning would have depressed the spirit of the strongest man or woman:

> The matchless piers, arcades, and clerestories of the nave, chancel, and aisles were lying on the ground in long piles of broken masonry. The encircling outer walls of all the chapels and the sanctuary stood in an unbroken line, completely encircling the ruins.

To the credit of the provost and the people gathered about him, the work of reconstruction, renewal and forgiveness began almost immediately. The cathedral

The destruction photographed soon after the air raid on the night of 14 November 1940; note the buckled metal flitch plates from the roof that may have contributed to its collapse

FAR RIGHT: *The charred cross, made from surviving timbers three months after the destruction and placed near the new altar in the apse, has become a globally recognised symbol of renewal after destruction*

BELOW: *A service in the ruins, 1945; much of the rubble lies where it fell, but an area has been cleared over the west and east crypts and the floor capped with concrete to prevent water penetration*

very quickly acquired a new and potent symbolic meaning, epitomised by the erection of the charred cross made from roof timbers. Soon after the raid, and continuing up to 1958, the Wyley Chapel in the east crypt began to be used for the celebration of Holy Communion. With no building above to protect it, water began to leak through the groined vault. Provost Howard eventually arranged for a concrete cap to be laid on the floor of the ruined church above and 'a reasonable degree of comfort was achieved'. The concrete cover can clearly be seen in a photograph taken from the tower in 1945, capping the vaults of both crypts, while the rubble in the Lady/Drapers' Chapel remains undisturbed.

In January 1941 Jack Forbes, the mason who had built the new altar and sanctuary in 1937 and who had been one of the four firewatchers on duty on the night of 14 November, was asked by Howard to construct a new altar out of rubble on the site of the destroyed one. The symbolic charred cross, supported in a bucket of sand, was erected there soon after.

In March 1941 a fragment of wall painting, possibly portraying the face of Christ with the Madonna and Child, was discovered high up on the wall at the corner of the Girdlers' Chapel with the Drapers'/Lady Chapel. The painting (see p.44), later dated to about 1330, faced westwards, and had probably decorated the east jamb of the central window of the Chapel of the Virgin Mary on the Hill (c.1300).

On 17 March 1941 the Council of Coventry Cathedral, meeting for the first time since the night of the destruction, resolved to build a new cathedral on or near the site of the ruins. Advice and opinions were widely sought, most importantly from the Central Council for the Care of Churches. Their recommendations included the repair and retention of the outer walls of the ruined cathedral and the preservation of the spire as the predominant feature. On 9 March 1942 the Cathedral Council decided to rebuild on the existing site, incorporating what remained of the medieval church. The removal of the ruined walls was certainly discussed but, in a sympathetic response to the recommendations of the Central Council, it was concluded 'that it would be wrong to destroy such extensive and beautiful remains'. Proposals to leave the cathedral as a ruin and to enlarge Holy Trinity, or build on a new site, were roundly rejected. It was decided to appoint Sir Giles Gilbert Scott as architect. He was the nephew of John Oldrid Scott, who had restored St Michael's in 1885–90, and his mastery of neo-Gothic, shown to great effect in Liverpool's Anglican cathedral, was much admired by Provost Howard.

While the plans for rebuilding were being discussed, a number of smaller works were executed in the ruins. During the winter and spring of 1941–42 the south porch was converted into a chapel for visitors, the ribbed vault and walls made safe and watertight and a small stone altar installed. The new chapel was dedicated in June 1942 by Mervyn G. Haigh, Coventry's third bishop (1931–42) and named the Chapel of the Resurrection.

Other works carried out at this time included the erection of a small, stone mono-pitch structure over the top of the stairs leading down into the Wyley Chapel. Its function, apart from possible blast protection, was to prevent rainwater running down the stairs and flooding the chapel. A timber kiosk was erected beneath the tower to serve as an office and provide a stall for the sale of literature and the receipt of donations. Three narrow paths were eventually cut through the rubble, running parallel to the 'open way' to the sanctuary, cleared in 1941.

Early in 1945, the bishop and provost offeered the west crypt to the Joint Council of the Coventry Christian Service Centre, to serve as a temporary Chapel of Unity. 'This very damp and dark chamber was transformed into a well-ventilated, well-warmed and brightly-lit chapel, holding about a hundred people.' Jack Forbes laid a stone floor, using material sent from Lichfield, and on 14 November 1945, the fifth anniversary of the 'Great Raid', the west crypt was dedicated as part of a grand ceremony of commemoration. The project also involved excavating the floor of the Girdlers' Chapel to unblock the ancient north doorway of the crypt. The purpose was to provide access directly from the ruins to the new Chapel of Unity, the work starting in late 1945 and completed in October of the following year. A stone porch with a door was then built over the staircase to protect it from the elements.

The old cathedral and the new

During October and early November 1947 the rubble, now overgrown with vegetation, was transported out of the ruins. It was noted during the operation that 'practically nothing of interest was found among the debris, everything having been destroyed in 1940', not a conclusion that would be reached today. It appears that not all the stone was removed from the site, however; the crypt now known to be immediately east of the Wyley Chapel is full of stone rubble, which can only have been deposited from above. It is possible, therefore, that part of the roof vault collapsed during the removal of the debris and that the opportunity was taken to fill the void with stone.

The design proposed by Sir Giles Gilbert Scott laid a new cathedral from north to south across the medieval church, with the apse surviving as an eastern projection. It was controversial, more because of its traditional style than for the proposed destruction of the fabric of the old cathedral. In November 1946 the Royal Fine Arts Commission recommended that the design be abandoned. Scott resigned at the beginning of January 1947 and the Harlech Commission

The ruins in the early 1950s, with the rubble removed and lawns and pathways laid out

The old and new cathedrals are linked by Basil Spence's massive canopy

was appointed to 'hear evidence and advise on the provision of a cathedral church'.

In the autumn of 1950 the cathedral launched an architectural competition which received 219 entries. The designs submitted by Basil Spence of Edinburgh were selected in early August 1951; Spence regarded the aims of the reconstruction as twofold, the first being the building of the new cathedral and the second the preservation of St Michael's, so that old and new could be appreciated as a whole. His first concept placed the new building on a north-south axis, which partly overlapped the old cathedral and would have required the demolition of a section of the north wall. The plan was soon revised and the new building was set back, with a canopy providing the physical and symbolic connection between the two buildings. Unknown to Spence, the west side of his cathedral almost touched the buried foundations of the east chevet end of the medieval cathedral of St Mary, destroyed in the Reformation. The chevet, consisting of an apse, ambulatory and three radiating polygonal chapels, was unusual for an English cathedral. Thus Coventry's two earlier cathedrals were connected through the footprint of the third (see plan on p.16).

In July 1947 the Harlech Commission recommended that the cathedral ruins should be laid out with 'grass lawns, gravel aisles and hallowing places'. The work was contracted to the Parks Department of Coventry City Council and carried out between January and Easter 1948. The concrete capping over the west and east crypts and the stone 'porches' over the stairs to the Wyley Chapel and the stairs to the Chapel of Unity were left undisturbed. Six 'Hallowing Places' were established around the perimeter of the walls, a contemporary interpretation of the former guild chapels. Each of these consisted of an enclosure bounded by a low turf wall planted with flowers.

The cathedral walls, now exposed to the weather on all sides, needed urgent attention and a detailed report was submitted by Basil Spence at the end of April 1952. Fortunately he did not follow the advice of one contractor consulted over costs, who recommended 'extensive demolition and rebuilding'. Eventually Messrs J.R. Deacon of Lichfield were selected and the contract began on 26 August 1952. The bulk of the work was carried out to the interior sides of the surviving walls. The vulnerable apse was reinforced at top and bottom with a reinforced

As part of the early work of renewal, six 'Hallowing Places' were created round the perimeter of the cathedral as a contemporary interpretation of the earlier guild chapels

concrete 'girdle' and a deep concrete foundation respectively. The east window of the south aisle was completely rebuilt as a faithful replica of the earlier design. When the contract was finished, it was remarked that little could be seen for an expenditure of £10,000, a sign that the conservation of the ruins had been properly carried out.

Work on the new cathedral commenced in June 1954, while in the old cathedral the damaged effigy of Bishop Yeatman-Biggs was repaired and re-installed at the east end of the Lady/Drapers' Chapel, and unveiled on 20 June 1954. In September 1954 the Cappers' Company approved Spence's proposals for the reconstruction of the Cappers' Room, largely destroyed in the Blitz. J. R. Deacon again won the contract for the work, which was completed in April 1957 and dedicated in December by Bishop Bardsley.

The wall painting of the Madonna and Child discovered in 1941 was left covered with roofing felt over a wooden framework and in 1955 Edward Clive Rouse was appointed to provide advice on its conservation. Rouse did not consider the painting, which had deteriorated badly since its discovery, worthy of the effort of preservation *in situ* and an attempt was made to remove it. As it was attached to plaster only ¼ in (63mm) thick, it disintegrated. Luckily a full-sized copy had been made when it was found, which was later used as a design for a Christmas card.

In 1956 the third window from the east in the Lady/Drapers' Chapel was demolished and converted into a wide doorway, in order to provide a permanent link between the old and new cathedrals. On 2 March 1956 Queen Elizabeth II passed through the new opening, named the Queen's Way, in order to lay the foundation stone of the new cathedral.

In September 1958 the old timber kiosk at the bottom of the tower was replaced by a bookstall 'in contemporary style', designed by Basil Spence. In the

RIGHT: The Queen's *Way* in the early 1960s, awaiting the construction of steps to the new cathedral; note the temporary stone structure that protected the stairs leading down into the east crypt
BELOW: The Queen's *Way* today, leading from the Drapers' Chapel into the new cathedral

same month a timber pavilion, the Appeal Centre, funded by four local firms, was erected on the north-west side of the ruin. It was used as an exhibition space and to display items such as chairs and hassocks that could be purchased and donated to the new cathedral. In October 1960 the charred cross in the ruins was removed from the bucket of sand in which it had stood since 1940 and taken to the west crypt to be dried out and treated with preservative.

With the cathedral promoting the ministry of peace and reconciliation, the first International Centre was opened by the evangelical bishop of Berlin on 17 January 1960. The former coke house and the organ chamber below the south-east aisle were converted to a refreshment room and a reading room. A period of close co-operation between the cathedral and German churches had begun, which culminated in the restoration of the ruined vestries. These had remained derelict since 1940, having lost their roofs and windows in the air raid. A group of German carpenters, masons and engineers from Aktion Suhnezeichen (Action for Reconciliation), sponsored by Christian churches in Germany, arrived in October 1961 to undertake restoration work, which created an oratory, library, lounges and a canteen for an expanded International Centre. A young architect, Michael von Moellendorff, collaborated with his father Wolf, a well-known Berlin church architect, on the design, and all the materials and labour were funded from Germany. The new International Centre was officially opened on 15 April 1962, in good time for the consecration of the new cathedral on 25 May. A new copper-covered portico covered the old entrance from the south aisle through which the fire had burst to destroy the vestries in 1940.

The Chapel of Unity had already been moved to the completed undercroft of the new cathedral in

The south aisle and tower after restoration work was carried out in 2013

The 1886 vestry beneath the dramatic skeleton of the apse; the other three bays of the vestry are medieval

1959, and in July 1961 work began on the conversion of the west crypt into a choir room. As part of the conversion, the small stone entrance from the cathedral ruins was demolished and replaced with a low structure incorporating a ventilator. The corresponding entrance to the Wyley Chapel had been removed earlier and the staircase completely sealed off. The west crypt was re-dedicated as the Chapel of the Cross in 1962.

The erection of tiers of seats in the ruins for the consecration of the new cathedral (25 May 1962), and the resulting press of visitors, wore the lawns bare. More durable York stone paving was therefore laid in 1963 and is essentially the surface walked on by the visitor today. Drainage was included for the first time, requiring the floor levels to be raised. The extra material further helped to protect the precious archaeology of the cathedral floor, with one notable exception. During the contract a concrete mixer lorry arrived to deliver its load. It was too heavy for the roof of the unknown vault beneath to bear and it collapsed, dropping the lorry horizontally into the void. Only the top of the cab and the mixer could be seen. The collapse took place in the centre of the innermost north nave aisle. Apart from the west and east crypts, recent research has identified the location of about ten burial vaults within the cathedral floor and there are probably many more.

Spence's practice designed a new bookshop to replace the wooden hut in the ruins. In grey concrete, materials and form, contrasting with the cathedral ruins, it was erected in 1964 on the north side of the old cathedral. This position completely blocked the exterior elevation of the north porch.

Since the York stone paving was laid in 1963 there has been no significant alteration to the appearance of St Michael's. The drama of destruction, rebuilding and restoration was over, to be followed by a period of relative stability and consolidation. Much of the work has involved the more mundane, but no less important, maintenance of the friable sandstone fabric of the walls and tower and other routine tasks.

ECCE HOMO
ECCE
HOMO
DONATIONS
COVENTRY CATHEDRAL - LIVING ICON OF

OPPOSITE: *Jacob Epstein's massive and angular* Christ before Pilate, Ecce Homo, *sculpted in 1934–35 and placed in the ruins in 1969*
OVERLEAF: *Josefina De Vasconcello's* Reconciliation, *donated by Richard Branson and installed in 1995*

It is an unenviable task to keep a building without a roof in good condition and safe for visitors, but this also happens to be one of the three largest medieval churches in the country. If this were not enough, there is another cathedral, no longer new, that is also beginning to deteriorate.

The most prominent of the few new pieces introduced in this period is Jacob Epstein's *Christ Before Pilate*, sculpted in 1934–35, which was placed on the south side of the cathedral ruins in 1969. In the outer north aisle there is also a striking bronze of man and a woman kneeling in an embrace, entitled *Reconciliation*. It was sculpted by Josefina De Vasconcello, donated by Richard Branson and installed in 1995. Not so obvious, but a major undertaking in 1987, was the re-hanging in the lower part of the second stage of the tower of the 12 bells, allowing them to peal at long last. This work was largely financed through a donation from Lady Lyons, the widow of Sir William Lyons, founder of car firm Jaguar Cars. The ringing room is situated immediately above the Tourist Information Centre and the bells can be seen from a new viewing chamber, reached from a spiral staircase in the tower.

In the winter of 2002–3 the Blitz Museum was opened in the former International Centre, and the time has now arrived not only to commemorate one tragic and traumatic event in the life of St Michael's, but also to celebrate and interpret the many centuries of the cathedral's history. The medieval glass was returned several years ago to the undercroft of the new cathedral, where it has lain largely unseen. With the help of the World Monuments Fund, this glass is currently being cleaned, classified and re-assembled so that eventually it can be placed on display for all to appreciate. The east and west crypts have become increasingly damp and their use for worship has now ceased. The wider project seeks to find a new use for the crypts, so that this very early and hidden part of the cathedral can be visited once again by the public. New ideas are under discussion for changes within the old cathedral, for example revealing and using the north and south porches as entrances and exits. It is clear the cathedral's fascinating past can only be preserved by giving it a new and secure future. A historic building should not be changed before it is understood; it is hoped that this book will play its small part in that process.

St Michael's: The Medieval Stained Glass

1. The History of the Glass

On Michaelmas day 1451, St Michael's, Coventry formed the setting for a spectacular event: William Waynflete, then bishop of Winchester and the realm's pre-eminent prelate, accompanied by a body of splendidly apparelled priests and clerks, led a devoutly bareheaded Henry VI and many other lords in procession around the churchyard, before entering the church to conduct High Mass in the king's presence, culminating in Henry's ceremonial donation, as an altar cloth, of his 'gowne of gold tissu, furred with a furre of a marturn sabull'. The main body of St Michael's was, by the time of Henry's visit, almost certainly complete, transforming the church into one of the great urban monuments of the late Middle Ages. Constructed in the fashionable Perpendicular aesthetic, maximising window openings and minimising masonry to a thin grid of slender mullions and transoms, St Michael's gave particular prominence to stained glass. The gift, as we will see, of Coventry's wealthy elite, and involving some of the country's finest medieval glass painters, the glazing at St Michael's was characterised not only by quantity, but also by the diversity of its subject matter and, in parts, the exceptional quality of its execution.

Following Henry's visit, further opportunities for vitreous display were provided by the addition of chapels to the north and south sides of the nave of St Michael's, possibly completed c. 1500. But within just a few decades, the iconoclastic attentions of Protestant reformers turned to windows and other kinds of painting; legislation marking the accession of Edward VI in 1547 called for the removal and destruction of 'pictures, paintings and all other monuments of feigned miracles...so that there remain no memory of the same in walls, glass-windows, or elsewhere'. The immediate impact of the royal injunction on the windows of St Michael's is not clear. The representation of Coventry's social elite in the church's windows, through images of benefactors, donors and coats of arms, may have lent the medieval glass a continued relevance to its post-Reformation audience, and hence a measure of protection, and there is also evidence suggesting a degree of preservation of old rituals (see p. 51). Yet from the late fourteenth century onwards, when the Lollard movement first found support in the city, Coventry had been associated with resistance to aspects of church authority and Catholic doctrine. By the middle of the seventeenth century, St Michael's had been stripped of all 'superstitious' elements: the brass eagle was sold, the font taken down, inscriptions and crosses painted out.

In this context, the church's medieval glass cannot have fared well, although it is impossible to know whether it was deliberately destroyed (certainly the loss of much glass from the church was later attributed to 'over-zealous reformers') or simply subject to the same general neglect suffered by the fabric of the medieval church in the post-Reformation period. The eighteenth-century refurbishment of

The ruins of the east end of St Michael's, showing the reduction of masonry to, essentially, a frame for stained glass windows

Watercolour by Henry Jeayes, c.1800, showing the medieval glass still in place in the clerestory

St Michael's badly deteriorated interior placed little value on the then-unfashionable medieval glazing; at best, the stained glass remains were swept out of their various (perhaps original) windows and grouped together elsewhere. By the middle of the century the choir clerestory had been completely stripped of its glass, and the nave clerestory glazing was seriously depleted when the glass was collected and, supplemented by other newly purchased 'painted glass', placed in the apsidal windows of the church's east end – probably to form a backdrop to the fashionably classical altar piece put up in 1750 (see p.61). At worst, medieval glass was simply 'thrown away as mere rubbish', as was that rescued for his study by the rector of Stanford-upon-Teme (Worcs.) in 1782. In restorations at the church in the following century, the medieval glazing remains were disturbed again.

Beginning in the early 1850s, the three central windows of the apse were filled with modern glass in memory of Queen Adelaide, and the medieval glass pushed into the two outer windows. As was common in the period, the work was entrusted to local plumbers, rather than to a medieval stained glass specialist. As aesthetic taste moved away from the classical to a revived interest in Gothic forms, however, the value of St Michael's medieval glass became increasingly appreciated. The preparatory report by John Oldrid Scott in 1882 (see p.73) noted the quality of the glass and even considered attempting to restore portions of its original design,

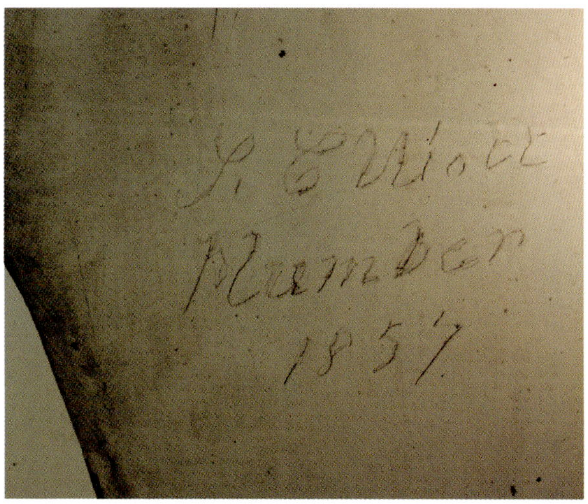

A fragment from St Michael's inscribed, S.C.Wott, plumber, 1857

although ultimately settled on cleaning, re-leading and re-inserting the painted glass, with more appropriate support.

In the early decades of the twentieth century, the stained glass at St Michael's (by now a cathedral) gained a place in the nascent academic study of England's medieval glass legacy, and in the early 1930s was professionally photographed by Sidney Pitcher. After the outbreak of war with Germany in September 1939, one of the first precautionary measures carried out by the cathedral was the removal of the surviving medieval panels from their windows in the apse and nave clerestory, into safe storage at Hampton Lucy rectory, a few miles north of Stratford-upon-Avon. The cathedral provost, R.T. Howard, noted that 'next to the fabric, the most important treasure of the Cathedral is its medieval glass'. On the night of 14 November 14 1940, that fabric was destroyed during the Blitz of the city, and its medieval glass collection found itself with no obvious home.

One of six medieval panels showing angelic figures standing on wheels, installed in the early 1980s in St Michael's Hall in the new cathedral at Coventry

Fortunately Sir Basil Spence had always envisaged the incorporation of some of the medieval glass into his new cathedral at Coventry, and in 1965 the first (and some of the best surviving) medieval fragments to be restored to Coventry were installed in the Haigh Chapel, within the ruins of St Michael's. The success of this display led, in the early 1980s, to the creation of seven more panels, by a team at the York Glaziers Trust, showing six figures of feathered angels standing on wheels, flanking a scene of the Resurrection, which were installed across the windows of St Michael's Hall. A decade later, the crates were opened again and six more panels created. The remains of three further seraphs were discovered and made up into panels, along with three 'mosaic' panels of some of the more interesting (largely figural) remaining fragments. Initially displayed in the offices of the insurance company Axa Equity & Law, a major employer in Coventry which funded the conservation work, these six new panels were ultimately put on display in the Chapel of Industry, Spence's first choice for housing the medieval glass remains.

The creation of these three sets of panels still left an enormous number of fragments loosely stored in their original packing crates until, in 2003, during the closure of the King & Son workshop in Norwich, which had made the first panels restored to the cathedral in 1965, a number of trays of forgotten fragments were discovered, some of them very fine. Initially sent for safe-keeping to Holy Well Glass in Wells, these were returned to Coventry in 2009, to purpose-built shelving in the new cathedral undercroft, finally reuniting all of St Michael's medieval glass remains. Three years later, the inclusion of the former cathedral church on the World Monuments Watch of imperilled historic sites threw a comprehensive spotlight on St Michael's medieval stained glass legacy, leading to a programme of cleaning, recording and documentation of the remains, as well as discussions as to their physical display. After almost three-quarters of a century spent, for the most part, in the dark, the St Michael's collection re-emerged as a source for understanding the medieval church, its patrons and donors, and the glass painters responsible for its production.

2. The iconography of the fifteenth-century glazing scheme

This eventful, and frequently destructive, history is one that would never have been imagined by those responsible for glazing St Michael's in the fifteenth century. The glass, like all medieval religious glazing, was intended as a permanent memorial, a way of capturing forever the wishes and beliefs, the ideas and aspirations, of the individuals and groups who had designed and paid for it. The damages and loss, reorganisation and ultimate removal from both its windows and (for the most part) the leads that bound it into panels, suffered by the glass, obscure significantly the nature of the original glazing scheme at St Michael's. Nonetheless, a number of themes dominate.

Angels and patrons

Representations of angels pervaded medieval art, announcing God's will, protecting, punishing and guiding man. Frequently shown in universally popular scenes such as the Annunciation, Nativity, Adoration of the Magi, Crucifixion, Resurrection and Last Judgement, angels were also deployed

FAR LEFT: *Angel bearing a shield of the arma Christi, showing the five wounds of Christ, from St Michael's, now in Coventry Cathedral's Chapel of Industry*
LEFT: *Angel musician with harp (fragment 034/035), from St Michael's*

The remains of a devil in the pan of a balance, from an image of St. Michael (fragments 017/016 and 122/017)

liberally in stained glass as censor bearers, candle holders or simple adorers, often within tracery openings, flanking and increasing the heavenly associations of saintly or Christological subjects. Angels were also regularly used as the bearers of shields of arms, both in the form of the *arma Christi* and secular heraldry. From the thirteenth century onwards, angel musicians became an increasingly popular feature of stained glass, particularly in the context of Marian subjects, such as the Assumption and Coronation of the Virgin.

There is evidence that angels appeared in the fifteenth-century glazing scheme at St Michael's in many of these, and other, contexts; in doing so they underscored and expanded on subjects elsewhere in the church's decorative scheme. Figures of angels decorated the tie-beams of the medieval choir roof, for example, while some of the roof corbels in the Drapers'/Lady Chapel incorporated angels bearing shields. Such a proliferation of angelic imagery can probably be associated with the church's dedication to St Michael the Archangel, who appears to have been represented in a range of glass imagery at St Michael's.

An image of the Last Judgement was incorporated into the fifteenth-century glazing (many of the surviving fragments are now installed in the Haigh Chapel), and probably included a depiction of St Michael weighing the souls of the dead, as in near-contemporary examples at Ticehurst, East Sussex (c.1425–50), Great Malvern Priory, Worcs. (c.1440), Thornhill, W. Yorks. (early 1490s), and, most splendidly, in the west window of Fairford parish church in the early sixteenth century.

Two fragments surviving from St Michael's, showing a small devil in the pan of a balance (against which souls were weighed) are unlikely to have belonged to the Judgement imagery. The architectural elements behind the white cords from which the pan hangs suggest the angel saint was here represented as a stand-alone figure housed within an architectural niche, and it is possible that he appeared in the context of his fellow archangels. One inscribed fragment appears to read 'Urael', perhaps a variation of the Archangel Uriel's name. At the end of the fifteenth century, Michael and Uriel, with Gabriel and Raphael, were depicted flanking a visual representation of a canticle of the Virgin, at Great Malvern Priory, dedicated jointly to SS Mary and Michael.

The expansion of the iconography of St Michael into a treatment of the Nine Orders of Angels was almost certainly a feature of the fifteenth-century Coventry scheme. Various medieval authors had attempted to identify and define angels and their role in God's divine governance, but most influential was the Pseudo-Dionysius's *De Hierarchia Celesti* of c.500, in which angels were classified into three hierarchies each containing three choirs:

the highest comprising Cherubim, Seraphim and Thrones; the middle, Dominations, Virtues and Powers; and the last, Principalities, Archangels and Angels. Although there seems to have been little consensus on the precise depiction of each of the individual orders, certain iconographic tendencies in the medieval portrayal of the various orders are discernible. Particularly distinctive were the orders of Principalities and Dominations, shown as angelic figures in royal robes, and with weapons, as a sign of Principalities presiding over kingdoms, or, for Dominations, with princely attributes, such as crowns, sceptres and swords. It is probable, therefore, that a number of fragments from St Michael's showing portions of feathered limbs or wings against ermine garments have their origins in representations of one of these orders, as may a partial head belonging to a golden-haired, clean-shaven crowned figure. This is comparable with representations of Dominations and Principalities elsewhere, while

OPPOSITE: *The delicate window tracery in which the medieval glass was set*

Partial head, possibly belonging to an image of one of the Nine Orders of Angels, from St Michael's (fragment 038/025)

Head probably from a representation of one of the angelic Orders, from St Michael's (fragment 034/039)

royal figures and saints tended in this period to be shown as mature figures, grey haired and bearded. Another head, showing a haloed figure with flowing golden locks wearing an elaborately decorated padded chaplet, bears strong similarities to some contemporary depictions of several of the angelic orders, such as those of Principalities, Powers and, in particular, Cherubim on the spectacular rood screen featuring the Nine Orders at Barton Turf, in Norfolk.

The theological complexity of the Nine Orders, the uncertainty and obscurity of some of the hierarchies, contributed to a relative lack of widespread popular interest in the orders in their entirety. But at St Michael's it is possible that they appeared more than once. As well as fragments of large-scale figures, the St Michael's collection also includes smaller-scale fragments. One, for example, shows a feathered arm holding a gold shaft against a feathered torso, resembling the Cherubim in the tracery lights of the nave clerestory at Great Malvern Priory, while fragments of wings of multi-eyed peacock feathers, traditionally also denoting Cherubim, are found throughout the St Michael's collection.

If the angelic orders did appear on both a monumental and a smaller scale in the St Michael's glazing, the decision to represent them in such a prominent manner was no doubt associated with the church's patron saint. It was under his day, 29 September, that one of the most influential books of the later Middle Ages, the compendium of saints' lives and of liturgical and doctrinal instruction known as the *Legenda Aurea*, described and considered the various orders in most depth. In stained glass, where the orders nearly always appeared in the subordinate position of tracery lights, the only other known example of both a full-sized series and one occupying smaller tracery openings in the same church is at Great Malvern Priory, where St Michael also served as a patron saint. At St Michael's itself, before the destruction of the church in 1940, coving attached to the roof beam above the rood, where the chancel met the nave, was decorated with a painting of St Michael overcoming Satan, below an inscribed list and descriptions of the Nine Angelic Orders.

The prominence of imagery at St Michael's associated with the church's patron saint may also have been prompted by a broader association with St Michael in Coventry. By 1351, and until the early seventeenth century, the common seal of Coventry depicted on its reverse an image of St Michael slaying the dragon alongside the legend (in translation) 'the communal seal of the town of Coventry'. That St Michael's was an expression of the pious benefaction of the same dominant ruling class in Coventry which used the town's common seal perhaps made pronounced imagery of St Michael within the church's glazing particularly appropriate.

Cherubim from the Nine Orders rood screen at Barton Turf (Norfolk), early fifteenth century

Donors and their education

Coventry's wealthy elite and their interests were certainly represented in other respects at St Michael's. The traditional attribution of the church's west tower, begun in the 1370s, to Adam and William Botoner, brothers who were both at various times mayors of Coventry, alongside records of gifts and benefactions towards building works by other local figures into the 1500s, illustrates the role of Coventry's elite in transforming the church into a monument of architectural magnificence. It is similarly evident that lay benefactors and donors were also firmly involved in the church's stained glass. From the thirteenth century onwards, donors and benefactors were frequently depicted in stained glass, following, by *c.* 1400, a basic formula of a kneeling figure, hands raised in prayer or praise, generally housed at the foot of a window, sometimes alongside members of their families, or set before prayer desks in increasingly elaborately furnished interiors.

The best-surviving examples of these so-called 'donor' figures from St Michael's recognisably depict variations of this type. One shows the remains of a male figure, his head lost, but dressed in a rich blue gown with fur cuffs, kneeling in prayer on a chequer-board tiled floor, before a desk holding both an inscribed prayer scroll and a string of rosary beads, against a decorative 'damask' curtain or hanging. Over his head arches a (fragmentary) scroll inscribed with his prayer, to which the words '*Filius dei*' '*mate(r)*', '*Christi*' appear to belong. Another, dressed in a similar gown and wearing the 'pudding bowl' hairstyle characteristic of lay donors of the first half of the fifteenth century, perhaps provides an indication of his fellow citizen's original appearance. In the Haigh Chapel are set the remains of a group of four female donors, elegantly dressed in blue, muslin-collared gowns, gold belts with floral badges, and high horned headdresses with jewel-pinned veils. A second group of three similarly-attired women, kneeling with their hands in prayer against a foliage ground, was recorded in the north nave clerestory of St Michael's prior to the removal of the church's glass in 1940. These may possibly represent mothers with their daughters, or perhaps more probably, given their similar costumes, may commemorate acts of 'corporate' gift-giving, perhaps as the wives of guild members.

In addition to these relatively well-preserved figures, there are scores of partial remains – heads, hands raised in prayer, prayer desks and rosary beads – almost certainly belonging to similar subjects. A number of directly comparable remains probably suggest sequences of figures to the same designs occupying windows in different parts of the church. Direct indications of the individual identities of

RIGHT: *Kneeling male 'donor' figure from St Michael's (now in panel 115)*
BELOW LEFT: *Group of female 'donor' figures, now in the door screen of the Haigh Chapel*
BELOW RIGHT: *Partial figure, probably from 'donor' imagery, from St Michael's (now in panel 110)*

Wenceslaus Hollar's engraving of the coats of arms in the windows of St Michael's, from Dugdale's Antiquities of Warwickshire

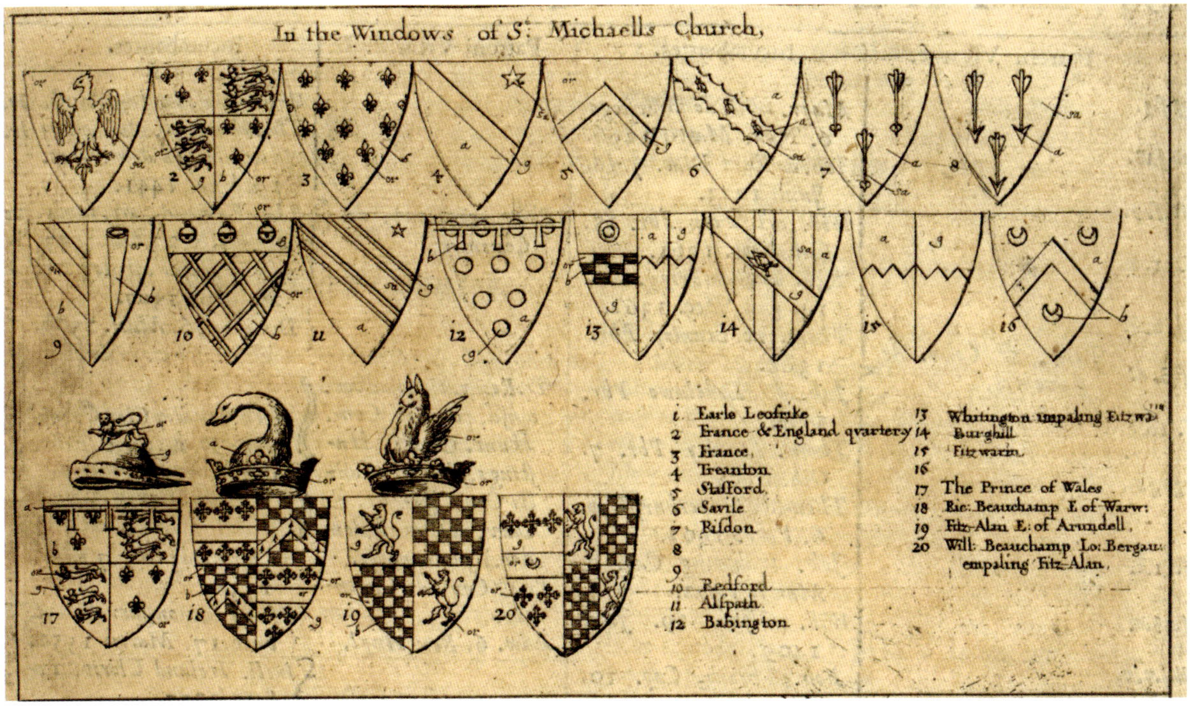

these donors or benefactors are rare, although the near-30 coats of arms identified and recorded, collectively, by William Dugdale and later by Thomas Sharp in the St Michael's windows, of which only fragments survive, may provide evidence. Certainly at other sites, the identity, marriages and alliances of individuals represented as donors at the foot of a window were advertised in the form of heraldry set within the same window's tracery openings.

A number of the shields of arms at St Michael's related to members of Coventry's Trinity Guild in the period of the construction and glazing of St Michael's. Among these are Henry VI (represented by the arms of France and England quarterly); the Prince of Wales; Richard Beauchamp, earl of Warwick (with his wife and son); William Beauchamp, Lord Abergavenny and his wife; Humphrey Stafford, 1st duke of Buckingham and various members of the local Stafford family. The Bedford arms may relate to guild members Thomas Bedford and his wife, Alicia. A Richard Alspathe and wife, as well as a 'Thomas de Alspathe, capellanus', are listed in the guild register, along with chief justice Sir William Babington and four-times mayor of London Richard Whittington and their wives, and Bishop John Burghill. With St Mary's Guildhall lying directly adjacent to St Michael's, it is more than possible that at least some of these figures bought themselves a place in the church's glazing scheme. Certainly, members of the guild are known to have contributed to St Michael's in other ways. Mayor John Crosse built the font, and is also credited with beginning the rebuilding of St Mary's.

It seems less likely that figures such as the Prince of Wales or Henry VI would have been direct benefactors to the parish church. The presence of their coats of arms in the glass at St Michael's indicates, therefore, that heraldic display at the church functioned in ways other than a simple record of gift giving, working iconographically to suggest a community of high-status supporters associated with the church. Indeed, it was perhaps the opportunity to become part of such a community that prompted benefaction by less-elevated donors at St Michael's, serving to preserve and advertise social ties and status, and bringing membership of a different, idealised community where the barriers of time and social rank temporarily dissolved within the context of the church windows.

A prominent theme of the iconography of the stained glass scheme at St Michael's seems to have been subjects of an educational nature. A concern for the instruction of the laity in the principles of Christian religion had occupied the church in

OPPOSITE: *A few small sections of the Victorian glass survives in some windows*

England since Archbishop Pecham's provincial Council of Lambeth in 1281 had set down its guide to Christian practice and belief, known as the *Ignorantia Sacerdotum*. Based around the Apostles' Creed, Lord's Prayer, Hail Mary and Decalogue, with an emphasis too on the Seven Sacraments, works of mercy, vices and virtues, the guide was to be expounded to parishioners four times each year, and its continued relevance is demonstrated by its continual reissue until the Reformation itself.

Teaching the catechism to a largely illiterate laity took place only partly from the pulpit; pictorial versions of the articles of the Faith propounded in *Ignorantia Sacerdotum* were frequently produced in wall-painting, stained glass and font sculpture. The remains of an Apostles' Creed on similar lines to other examples found in English glass of the fifteenth century, are the clearest evidence for a concern with catechetical education at St Michael's, surviving as a badly damaged, partially-haloed head, with remains of the grey hair and beard characteristic of late medieval depictions of the Apostles, and traces of a probable hat hanging at the back of the neck, indicating St James the Great as a pilgrim. A photograph by Pitcher of a panel then in the south nave clerestory shows the same head above a mosaic of fragments, including a quantity of white drapery pieces consistent with contemporary representations of the Apostles; in close proximity (at the bottom of the panel) to a portion of garment decorated with a scallop shell; and surrounded by pieces of an inscribed scroll, to part of which the extended finger of a hand emerging from beneath a white mantle points. It is these inscribed fragments that are most telling. Reading '*...ui / con..eptus*' and '*spiritu*', they are part of the sentence in the Creed attributed to St James the Great, '*qui conceptus est de spiritu sancto natus ex maria virgine*'.

Other possibilities for catechetical education are also suggested. Among the remains of representations of laymen and women in the St Michael's collection are fragments which cannot confidently be attributed to 'donor' figures, kneeling in prayer. One group of fragments, in particular, showing pairs of heads painted on the same piece of glass, recalls, instead, contemporary depictions of the Sacraments, Works of Mercy, Vices and Virtues, in which groups of lay figures crowd together to populate scenes designed to advise, instruct or warn. This is particularly so where the figures are shown with eyes clearly downcast, in observation of events (baptism, for example, or tending to the sick or naked) taking place before them. The survival of two further fragments suggests that a Seven Sacraments window, in which representations of each of the sacraments of Baptism, Confirmation, Matrimony, Eucharist, Penance, Holy Orders and Extreme Unction were grouped around an image either of the Crucifixion or of Christ showing his Passion wounds, was incorporated into the St Michael's scheme. In the first, a figure in a white garment supports a gold chrismatory of gabled design in his right hand, and opens the lid with his left to reveal vials of holy oil. Chrismatories also appeared in other contexts, such as representations of the order of Virtues in the fifteenth century, but the lack of evidence for a feathered body, with which Virtues were commonly depicted, suggests this was not the case with this fragment. It may instead come from a representation of the sacraments of Orders or of Confirmation, where the chrismatory is held by a cleric. In the second fragment, hands are laid on the head of a man, reflecting the gesture of the bishop

Eight Apostles with Creed scrolls, early fifteenth century, probably originally from Hereford Cathedral, now in the Museum of Fine Art, Boston

Remains of St James the Great, from an Apostles' Creed at St Michael's, photographed in the 1930s by Sidney Pitcher

ABOVE: *Heads of a pair of laymen (fragment 038/040), from St Michael's*
RIGHT: *Partially gabled chrismatory, held open to reveal vials of holy oil (fragment 044/017), from St Michael's*

in scenes of ordination, but here, given the lack of any evidence of a tonsure, perhaps more probably representing the sacrament of Penance.

The fragmentary and fragmented nature of the stained glass remains at St Michael's make it impossible to know whether articles of the catechism other than the Apostles' Creed and the Seven Sacraments were represented in the church's windows. Some institutions contained multiple articles; in the north choir aisle at Great Malvern Priory, for example, were the Seven Sacraments, an Apostles' and Prophets' Creed, the Decalogue and the Lord's Prayer, and it has been suggested that this part of the church may have served as an educational space for 'boys' or 'clerks'. Although inevitably speculative, it is worth considering that a basic form of education also took place at St Michael's. One striking fragment shows the remains of two inscribed lines, in two columns. The left-hand column contains the numbers 'XI' and 'XIX'; the right, the letters 'l' and 't', picked out in gold from a painted ground, and each surrounded by a cusped design, showing that they are not part of longer inscriptions. The fragment suggests a larger composition of a numbered alphabet. In its medieval version, which elided the letters 'i' and 'j', the eleventh letter was 'l' and the nineteenth 't'. With only one letter for the modern letters 'u' and 'v', a medieval alphabet is likely to have been represented with 24 letters, fitting neatly into a composition of three lines, with eight letters and numbers in each, in which the number XI and letter 'l' would sit directly above number XIX and the letter 't'.

The existence of an alphabet in stained glass in a mid-fifteenth century chantry chapel at the parish

ABOVE LEFT: *Detail from the scene of Orders in the Seven Sacraments window at Doddiscombleigh (Devon), late fifteenth century*

ABOVE RIGHT: *Fragment showing hands laid on the head of a layman (039/018), from St Michael's, perhaps representing the sacrament of Penance*

LEFT: *Fragment (094/008) inscribed with numbers and letters, possibly from a numbered alphabet at St Michael's*

church of St Mary at North Leigh, Oxfordshire, has been related to a fashion for the patronage of education, particularly after the establishing of Eton College in 1440 and King's College, Cambridge, in 1441 by Henry VI to mark his majority. In the context of the proliferation of chapel and chantry foundations at St Michael's in the late Middle Ages, it is not difficult to imagine that one such patron included provision for some kind of elementary education in the church, or that one or more of the 20 or so priests supported there was able to carry out such lessons. As well as helping to educate local children, such provision would have benefitted the founder through the prayers for his or her soul the children would have been expected to recite.

Stories of Christ and the saints

The most complete surviving main-light panel of stained glass from St Michael's represents Christ's Resurrection. Following the typical fifteenth-century formula, Jesus, wearing a crown of thorns and holding a pennoned cross-staff, steps out of a tomb-chest, around which are four sleeping soldiers; the scene is set against a ruby ground, below an architectural canopy. The form and scale of the panel suggest that the scene was originally part of a sequence of images narrating the story of Christ's Passion, a type of glazing to which numerous other elements of the St Michael's remains seem also to have belonged. Partial scenes of the Scourging of Christ (now in the Haigh Chapel), and possibly the Crucifixion, survive alongside more fragmentary traces of Passion subjects of comparative scale, including the Betrayal; the Agony in the Garden of Gethsemane; the Nailing to the Cross; and a figure group probably from the Harrowing of Hell.

The duplication of some iconographic details indicating the Betrayal, Scourging, Crucifixion and Resurrection, painted in a variety of styles, may suggest that more than one narrative of the Passion was incorporated into the medieval scheme at St Michael's. Although the narrative mode was not the only one through which Christological subjects were represented at the church (there is evidence of larger images of Christ Resurrected or Triumphant, and in Judgement), other kinds of stories relating to the life of Christ may also have been displayed in the windows at St Michael's. For example, some of the fragments showing Christ (without his crown of thorns) in the company of the Apostles, and groups of Apostles alone, may originally have belonged to scenes showing episodes from Christ's ministry and miraculous works.

Another possibility for some of these Christological remains is an origin in broader Christo-Marian cycles. With a cult coming second only to that of Christ himself, and Englishmen of the period encouraged to think of their country as being in a special way 'Mary's Dowry', the Virgin was

The Resurrection, St Michael's Hall, Coventry Cathedral, from St Michael's

LEFT: *Judas kissing Christ (fragment 037/030), from a scene of the Betrayal at St Michael's*
BELOW: *One of a number of groups of Apostles' heads (fragment 037/040) from the St Michael's fragments*

RIGHT: *One of a series of monograms of the Virgin (now on tray 119), from St Michael's*
FAR RIGHT: *Head of a virgin saint (now set in panel 118) from St Michael's*
BELOW: *Partial inscription, reading* 'Gaud(e) V(ir)go Mater', *now in panel 107 of the St Michael's fragments*

represented more than any other saint in English medieval art. In stained glass of the fifteenth-century, scenes from her life commonly accompanied representations of episodes from the life of Christ. The same combination of narrative cycles appeared on a form of winged, carved altarpiece produced in the Netherlands for the mass market from around 1380. It is tempting to speculate that the striking polygonal apse at the east end of St Michael's may have been envisaged as just such a retable in monumental form, its windows (the central trio, in particular, perhaps) filled with narratives of the lives of Christ and his mother as an enormous triptych.

Whether or not Marian iconography featured as an adjunct to Christological narrative at St Michael's in exactly this way, the Virgin was evidently a significant and, it seems, elaborately configured element of the church's original glass iconography. The glazing remains include roundels bearing the monogram of the Virgin; a partial inscription reading 'Virg…' of a size suggesting an origin in a label identifying a large-scale image of the Virgin; numerous portions of figures, some exceptionally finely painted, consistent (although not exclusively so) with contemporary representations of Mary; and fragments indicating the Marian-related iconography of St Anne teaching the Virgin to read.

Other remains suggest, perhaps strikingly in a parochial context, the presence of pictorial versions of Marian prayers and hymns, perhaps originally housed in the Lady Chapel that formed the north choir aisle. A number of fragments contain partial inscriptions apparently invoking and praising the Virgin. The most complete reads '*Gaud(e) V(ir) go Mater*', almost certainly originally '*Gaude Virgo Mater Christi*' ('Rejoice Virgin Mother of Christ'), suggesting a window illustrating one of the most popular medieval Latin hymns to the Virgin, narrating the major episodes (or 'Joys') of her life. Such windows are perhaps best known from the surviving scheme at Great Malvern Priory, in the north transept façade window of which is a series of 11 'Joys of Mary', from the Annunciation to the Coronation of the Virgin, accompanied below each scene by an appropriate

A fragment from an image of St Christopher, including lower legs wading through water, part of the Christ child's head and cross with pennant-banner, and portions of river bank, from St Michael's (now set in panel 145)

sentence beginning *Gaude*; and also from the now lost great *Gaude* window in an equivalent location at Canterbury Cathedral, where seven large pictures of the Virgin each had beneath it an inscription beginning *Gaude Maria*.

At Malvern, the *Gaude* was combined with the *Magnificat*, the Virgin's great prayer of thanksgiving and humility, based on Luke 1: 46–55. The survival from St Michael's of an inscribed fragment reading '*Et exulta*...' suggests the prayer was portrayed here too, reflecting the opening words of its second line, '*Et exultavit spiritus meus in Deo salvatore*' ('and my spirit has rejoiced in God my saviour').

The scores of partially haloed heads, male and female and of varying scales, surviving in the glass from St Michael's testify that the Virgin was by no means the only member of the holy company of Heaven occupying the church's windows. Although, for the most part, impossible to identify precisely, the distinctive iconography of the *Agnus Dei* and camel skin of St John the Baptist; the infant Christ born across the river by St Christopher; the spiked wheel of St Catherine; the scallop shell and pilgrim attire of St James the Great; and the pair of keys held by his bald-headed, short-bearded fellow Apostle, St Peter; are testimony to the presence of each of these saints, sometimes in multiple instances, in the glazing scheme at St Michael's. The treatment of these figures evidently varied. The St Christopher fragments closely follow contemporary examples of stand-alone images. Two fragments, together almost certainly showing St Catherine imprisoned, however, suggest that episodes from her vita, at least, were illustrated in the church's glass to some extent, perhaps as part of a longer narrative of her life; potentially in the context of the chapel at St Michael's known, in the Middle Ages, to have been devoted to her.

Two fragments (one set in panel 143, the other fragment 039/007), probably belonging to the same scene of St Catherine imprisoned, from St Michael's

3. Glaziers at St Michael's

The extended narrative cycles that seem to have been a marked feature of the St Michael's scheme became enormously popular in English stained glass of the fifteenth century, but the early use of the glazing form is strongly and particularly associated with one glazier, John Thornton of Coventry. Among the most accomplished and prolific of England's late medieval glass painters, Thornton is known through the contract he made in December 1405 with the dean and chapter at York to glaze the minster's great east window, filling it with an extensive Apocalypse cycle that differed dramatically from other recent high-status commissions, characterised by series of large standing figures within fictive niches.

Head from St Michael's (fragment 040/042) painted in the style of John Thornton

That Thornton was connected with the glazing of St Michael's seems clear. Partial figures of God the father, angels (see pp. 101 and 102), men and women painted in his style survive across the fragment collection, some ranking alongside any of those in the minster east window in terms of composition and subtlety. There are similarities too in details of design and composition: in decorative detailing, in distinctive foliage forms, and, perhaps especially, in the small figures set within niches in architectural side-shafting, characteristic of glass in Thornton's style across York. More difficult to establish is the extent and nature of Thornton's relationship with St Michael's. While the vast majority of the surviving fragments probably belong to the first half of the fifteenth century, they are strikingly varied in their painting style. Many retain points of contact with Thornton's style. In some, the delineation of faces is still characterised by large, round eyes; long noses

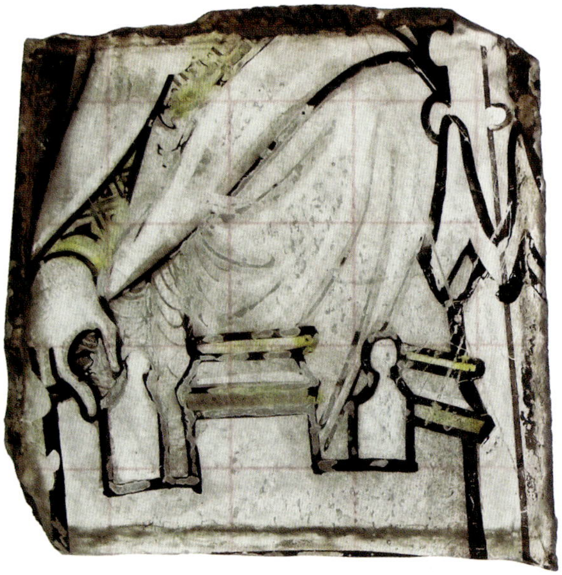

LEFT: *Partial figures in architectural contexts (fragments 034/020 and /001), almost certainly from the side-shafts of architectural framing at St Michael's*

BELOW: *Partial head of a cleric (fragment 036/014) from St Michael's, painted in a harder version of Thornton's style*

with bulbous tips; and small, pursed mouths; but the modelling is heavier, and the trace lines applied more forcefully and in greater quantity, resulting in a harder, less 'sculptural' appearance. In others, the features have lost some of the 'sweetness' (lent by small, full mouths, and wide rounded eyes, for example) characteristic of much of the glass closely associated with Thornton, replaced, instead, by heavy eye-lids, sometimes cutting straight across the eye; and wider, less pouting, mouths.

Alongside fragments such as these are other groups from St Michael's with less apparent connection to a Thornton manner of painting. The remains of figures of Christ and Judas from the Betrayal (see p.114), a probable angel wearing a jewelled chaplet (see p.104), and a crowned male saint, represent a particularly sensitively-painted group. Their well-proportioned faces have shorter noses, smaller, oval-shaped eyes and wider mouths than those associated with Thornton. The style also seems to incorporate an inclination towards elaborate detailing. The gold-rayed cross-halo of Christ and the arcaded halo of the king, for example, differ considerably from the simpler designs, of white haloes with plain gold or (typically) trefoil-cusped borders, seen in Thornton-style work. Equally distinctive, but very different in appearance, is a style characterised technically by an aggressive use of paint wash, linear shading and needle-work to create a heavily modelled appearance

Head of St Peter (fragment 034 from St Micha showing stylist with Thornton

Partial head of a male saint, probably crowned (fragment 035/009), from St Michael's

(see p.114, bottom image). Unusually, series of short, parallel lines are used to suggest both fullness (as above nostrils, and along upper lips) and shadow, such as in eye sockets. Eyebrows of mature males are wildly bushy; haloes appear mostly to be simply cusped.

How, then, should these differences in painting style be interpreted? The variations must, to some degree, be associated with the probable dates of the church's glazing. Apart from the west tower, begun in the 1370s, which perhaps had little opportunity for glazing, the rebuilding campaign for the main body of the church potentially spanned the six decades from c.1390 to c.1450. Stylistic change in stained glass over this period was significant, witnessing the introduction, dissemination and decline of the so-called International Gothic style.

With regard to Thornton, in particular, it is unlikely that he could have personally been involved in the glazing of the nave at St Michael's, whose windows were probably produced in the 1440s. Already undertaking a significant commission in 1405, the last known reference to him dates to Christmas Eve, 1433, when the dean and chapter at York made repairs to a house belonging to him. Indeed, while Thorntonesque in manner, much of the glass surviving from St Michael's is painted in a coarser, harder style, more linear and lacking in modelling; traits associated with the weakening of the International Gothic tradition from the late 1430s onwards. Thornton is known to have retained personal links with Coventry after his commission in York, almost certainly running a workshop out of his home city, and portions of the St Michael's glass were probably the product of glaziers active later than Thornton but with some connection, perhaps in their training or previous painting commissions, with him.

St Michael's choir, on the other hand, dating to c.1390–1420, falls squarely into the period during which Thornton was active and glass painted in his manner flourished; so it is noteworthy that only a relatively small proportion of the extant glazing from St Michael's is painted in a style fully recognisable as Thornton's, on the basis of his documented commission at York. But the extent of Thornton's involvement may now partly be obscured by his probable working practices. The terms of the 1405 York contract make it clear that he was expected to function not only as a glass painter, but also as designer and project manager. Other monuments containing glass painted in Thornton's style suggest he was able to manage complex operations, involving both the deployment of multiple painters within a single window, and even the co-ordination of glass painters working in different styles within 'his' commission. It is possible, therefore, that Thornton's involvement at St Michael's was more pronounced than that suggested by the collection of essentially isolated, and often fragmentary, heads.

Equally, however, the relative paucity of extant material in a fully-fledged Thornton style from St Michael's may reflect the fact that Coventry was a significant centre for artistic activity; glaziers are recorded in the city from the thirteenth century onwards, and the names of seven of Thornton's likely contemporaries are known. At the end of the fourteenth century, when work on the choir of St Michael's was perhaps begun, Thornton may have been just one (perhaps exceptionally accomplished) of a number of successful glaziers employed by the church to undertake its stained glass scheme. Certainly, with the possible exception of some of the glazing of St Mary's Guildhall (built 1394–1414), there is little evidence in Coventry itself that the apparently extensive workshop responsible for so much stained glass in his manner across the West Midlands in the first few decades of the fifteenth century was in operation prior to Thornton's 1405 commission in York. One hypothesis, therefore, is that it was his success in York, showcasing to magnificent effect the skills of a perhaps relatively youthful glazier, that enabled Thornton to establish a workshop not only in his 'adopted' city, but in his home town as well. His achievements in the north may have given him an important edge on the competition in an artistically very successful city.

Partial head, possibly from an image of St John (fragment 038/043), representing a style group at St Michael's

The link between York and Coventry came through two principal figures associated with the glazing of the east window, Richard Scrope, archbishop of York, and Walter Skirlaw, bishop of Durham at the time of the glazing, who had both been bishop of Coventry and Lichfield at periods between 1385 and 1398; but this does not explain why Thornton, in particular, was selected in a city with a flourishing glass-painting industry. It seems inconceivable that he would have been employed without those responsible for the York window having seen at least some stained glass produced by him; and there are signs that it was work at St Michael's that may have served as his showpiece. Establishing the date at which glazing work began at St Michael's is difficult. There is little surviving material that can incontrovertibly be dated to 1405; but there are a number of potentially significant fragments. The collection includes a portion of a fourteenth-century border design known to have been used until the 1390s, possibly indicating a date for the glazing closer to the beginning of the suggested c. 1390–1420 choir date range. More significant, perhaps, are the small figures housed within the side shafts of architectural canopies, common, as already noted, both to St Michael's and to much work in Thornton's style at York from the minster's great east window onwards, but not evident in stained glass in Thornton's style in the West Midlands. This might suggest that the design trait was one used by

Thornton at St Michael's and subsequently taken by him to York, but not adopted by his colleagues or pupils in Coventry who would go on to serve patrons in the West Midlands.

If these fragments indicate that Thornton produced stained glass for St Michael's before undertaking the 1405 York commission, others may provide insight into why he was selected for the task. It was noted by Peter Newton that the sources for Thornton's painting style lay not in earlier Midlands work, but in the Oxford 'school' of glass painting, associated with Thomas Glazier of Oxford, between c. 1380 and 1410. In particular, he noted, some of the work at New College, and that at Winchester College, is generally similar to Thornton's in a number of respects: the subtle use of enamel wash to support the painted line, particularly in the treatment of heads; the use of 'seaweed' foliage backgrounds; even the incorporation of figures into side-shafting. Indeed, there are some strikingly close parallels between details of some of the St Michael's fragments and work by Thomas of Oxford. For example, the unusual irregular-shaped 'oyster shell' jewels or gemstones that are a feature of Thomas Glazier's work can be found

LEFT: *Detail of the Virgin, Winchester College Chapel by Thomas of Oxford* c. 1393
BELOW: *Partial head surviving from St Michael's (fragment* 036/021*), with a fillet decorated with 'oyster shell' jewels and pearl-encircled jewel motif*

in the St Michael's remains; in more than one instance, this gemstone motif was used at St Michael's in conjunction with a pearl-encircled jewel motif of exactly the kind featured at Oxford. Elsewhere, the halo of an unidentified (but probably martial) saint from St Michael's, apparently painted in the Thornton style, closely parallels the unusual cross-hatched design of the Virgin in Winchester College chapel.

Indeed, it is arguable that the painting style of some of these figures from Coventry more closely resembles work attributed to Thomas Glazier than to that typically described as in the Thornton style produced after the York east window. For example, some of the standing figures of angels holding inscribed banners, almost certainly from the choir at St Michael's, are painted with wider mouths, noses that are broader along their length but less bulbous at their tip, and with distinctly heavier 'eye bags' beneath their lower lids than typical of York work, but reflecting closely elements of figures such as the Virgin now in Merton College.

BELOW: *Detail of an angel from the choir of St Michael's, now in St Michael's Hall*
BOTTOM: *Detail of the Virgin, now in the east window of Merton College Chapel, by Thomas of Oxford*

Taken together, these points may suggest a close and particular link between Thornton, before he travelled to York, and Thomas of Oxford. The painting style introduced by Thomas of Oxford in elements of the glazing at New College in the 1380s, and more fully at Winchester in the following decade, signalled a turning point in the history of English glass-painting, introducing to it the International Gothic style which dominated European art in the period *c.* 1380–1420. Thornton would go on to became instrumental in disseminating International Gothic in the Midlands and the north, and it is worth speculating that if, in the 1390s, he was producing stained glass in this attractive new style in Coventry, this caught the eye of those involved in commissioning the minster east window. There is some suggestion that there was already a fondness for this style at York Minster, prior to Thornton's employment. Figures belonging to an Apostles' and Prophets' Creed installed in the minster choir clerestory, almost certainly in the 1390s by John Burgh, the minster's principal 'resident' glazier in the late fourteenth and early fifteenth centuries, bear close stylistic similarities not only with the later New College and Winchester College glass, but between a number of the prophets that the York and Oxford schemes have in common, the parallels including textual errors apparently introduced at Oxford and repeated in York.

The final factor in the selection of Thornton may perhaps lie in the narrative glazing mode with which he was intimately (and, it seems, initially, exclusively) associated in the early fifteenth century. This may have been particularly attractive at York, as it has been suggested that Archbishop Scrope was particularly concerned with the promotion of the northern church, and was involved in planning the glazing of the whole east end of the minster to include prominent windows dedicated to the great northern saints, William and Cuthbert. The narrative form of these windows at York may have been intended to reflect (and supersede) the thirteenth-century narrative cycles, such as those devoted to St Thomas Becket, at the church's southern rival, Canterbury. Thornton may therefore have presented an unusual and compellingly attractive proposition to the minster: a breathtakingly skilful painter working in the new International style, who was also a thrillingly innovative designer promising to meet a particularly complex set of demands. Given that it has been shown that narrative glazing was almost certainly a significant feature of the stained glass at St Michael's, and that glazing may well have been begun there prior to 1405, St Michael's may well have served as the show-case for his skills; the passport to York and his subsequent career as one of the most successful glaziers of the Middle Ages.

Acknowledgments

GENEROUS DONORS TO THE CONSERVATION OF ST MICHAEL'S INCLUDE:

The World Monuments Fund Paul Mellon Endowment for Architectural Conservation in Great Britain
The Aldama Foundation
American Express
ChurchCare
English Heritage
The Marc Fitch Fund
The Headley Trust
The Radcliffe Trust
The Dr Mortimer and Theresa Sackler Foundation
The Peter Stormonth Darling Charitable Trust
The 29th May 1961 Charitable Trust
Ms Gillian Watt
The Barbara Whatmore Charitable Trust
WREN

AUTHOR ACKNOWLEDGMENTS

For someone born and bred in Coventry, who witnessed the new cathedral rising slowly from its foundations alongside the old ruins, it has been a great privilege to have been able to contribute to this volume. First and foremost I must thank Jonathan Foyle, Former Chief Executive of World Monuments Fund Britain, without whom this book would not have been written. He saw the case for publishing both my conservation and archaeology plan and Heather Gilderdale Scott's work on the conservation of the medieval glass. His 'outsider's' enthusiasm for the heritage of Coventry and for the cathedrals area is infectious and the cathedral authorities needed no convincing to become partners in the publication, for which I am most grateful.

Many people have helped, not least my wife Toni Demidowicz, who aided me in my research and patiently read all versions of my text. The staff in local archives such as the History Centre, Warwick Record Office and Birmingham Archives provided much assistance in these trying times of continuous cuts in public expenditure. This is not to forget the volunteer staff of the Coventry Cathedral Archives, who provide access to such an important collection. Michael Clews, the cathedral architect, Tony Auty and the staff of Coventry Cathedral, Dr Linda Monckton of English Heritage, Dr Richard Morris, Chris Patrick, Coventry's conservation and archaeology officer, and Anthony Blee, Basil Spence's principal architect, have all shared their profession expertise and provided valuable information and help. Jessica Hodge, our editor, has worked unremittingly to keep the authors to schedule and help convert our reports into readable text.
George Demidowicz

The medieval stained glass of St Michael's, Coventry, came to my attention through doctoral research, and I have since been grateful for the enthusiasm and encouragement of those at Coventry Cathedral, and particularly Dr Mike Stansbie, whose excellent images of the extant glass first allowed a close appreciation of its riches. I am grateful, more recently, to the World Monuments Fund Britain for the opportunity to study the St Michael's glass at close quarters and to be involved in its programme of restoration work. My thanks go especially to George Demidowicz who has, during the course of the project, kindly and cheerfully shared his findings and thoughts on medieval St Michael's.
Heather Gilderdale Scott

Bibliography

1. Building

ARCHIVAL SOURCES

There is insufficient room to provide details on archival sources and the main repositories can only be listed. A comprehensive bibliography of such material, including published sources, can be found in the report, Demidowicz (2013), a copy of which has been lodged in the Coventry Cathedral Archives and the Coventry History Centre.

Library of Birmingham, Archives and Heritage Department
Coventry Cathedral Archive, new Cathedral undercroft
Coventry History Centre (Coventry Archives and Local Studies)
Herbert Art Gallery and Museum
Lambeth Palace Library, London
RIBA Drawings Collection, V&A, London
Warwick County Record Office

REPORT

Demidowicz, George, *Coventry Old Cathedral: A Conservation Plan: An Historical, Architectural, Archaeological Study of Old St. Michael's* (2013), for the World Monuments Fund

PRIMARY SOURCES, PUBLISHED

Appendix Part II to the Second Report of Commissioners of Inquiry: The Second Report of The Commissioners for Inquiring into the State of Large Towns and Populous Districts (1845)
Harris, Mary Dormer, *The Coventry Leet Book* (1907)
Toulmin Smith, Lucy, *Leland's Itinerary in England and Wales* (1964 edition), vol. 2

SECONDARY SOURCES

Astley, John, *The Monumental Inscriptions of the Parish Church of S. Michael, Coventry*, 1884
Bassett, Steven, 'Anglo Saxon Coventry and its Churches', *Dugdale Society Occasional Papers* 41, 2001
Brookes, Alfred, *St Michael's Church, Coventry Past and Present; Also a brief history of the City of Coventry*, c. 1906
Chatwin, Philip B., 'Early Coventry', *Transactions of the Birmingham Archaeological Society* 53, 1928, pp. 132–44
The Cathedral Church of St Michael Coventry, Gloucester, c.1937 and a wartime edition, copies in Coventry History Centre
Coss, Peter, *The Early Records of Medieval Coventry*, 1986
Demidowicz, George (ed.), *Coventry First Cathedral: The Cathedral and Priory of St Mary*, 1994
Demidowicz, George, 'Introduction: Coventry – A New Beginning?' pp. 3–4 in Demidowicz, 1994
Demidowicz, George, *A Guide to the Buildings of Coventry: An Illustrated Architectural History*, 2003
Demidowicz, George, 'The Development of St Mary's Hall, Coventry: A Short History', in Linda Monckton and Richard K. Morris (eds) *Coventry Medieval Art, Architecture And Archaeology in the City and Vicinity*, 2011, pp. 164–81
Demidowicz, George, and Johnson, Stephen, *A History of Caludon Castle, The Lords of the Manor of Caludon*, 2013
Duffy, Eamon, *The Stripping of the Altars: Traditional Religion in England 1400–1580*, 1992
Howard, R.T., *Guide to the Cathedral Church of St Michael, Coventry*, 1954
Howard, R.T., *Ruined and Rebuilt: The Story of Coventry Cathedral 1939–1962*, 1962
Monkton, Linda, 'St Michael's Coventry: The Architectural History of a Medieval Urban Parish Church', *The British Archaeological Association Conference Transactions* XXIII, 2011, pp. 135–63
Morris, Richard, *Churches in the Landscape*, 1989
Poole, Benjamin, *Coventry: Its History & Antiquities*, 1870
[Reader, William], *Description of St Michael's Church Coventry with the Inscriptions from the Monuments, Tombs &c and a List of Charitable Benefactors to that Church and Parish*, 1815, reprinted 1830 under author's name
Rodwell, Warwick, *The Archaeology of Churches*, 2012
Sharp, Thomas, *Illustrations of the History and Antiquities of St Michael's Church, Coventry From original and mostly unpublished Documents*, 1818
Sharp, Thomas [and] William George Fretton, *Illustrative Papers on the History and Antiquities of the City of Coventry... from original and mostly unpublished Documents... with Corrections, Additions, and a brief memoir of the Author*, 1871
Soden, Iain, *Coventry: The Hidden History*, 2005
Spence, Basil, *Phoenix at Coventry: The Building of a Cathedral*, 1964
Stevens, W.B. (ed.) *The Victoria County History of Warwick* 8, 1969, sections by Joan C. Lancaster, pp. 346–57
Thomas, John, *Coventry Cathedral*, 1987
Williams, H.C.N., *The Pictorial Guide to Coventry Cathedral*, 1962
Woodhouse, Frederick W., *Churches of Coventry: A Short History of the City & its medieval remains*, 1909

2. Glass

Chatwin, Philip Boughton, 'Stained Glass from Coventry Cathedral', *Transactions of the Birmingham Archaeological Society* 66, 1945–6, pp. 1–5
Dormer Harris, Mary (ed.), *The Coventry Leet Book*, London, 1907–13
_____, *The Register of the Guild of the Holy Trinity, St Mary, St John the Baptist and St Katherine of Coventry*, Oxford, 1935
Dugdale, William, *The Antiquities of Coventry*, Coventry, 1756
Howard, R.T., 'Faces in the Glass: A Note on the Discovery', *Coventry Cathedral Chronicle* 4, 1940
Heard, Kate, 'Death and Representation in the 15th Century: The Wilcote Chantry Chapel at North Leigh', *Journal of the British Archaeological Association* 154, 2001, pp. 134–49
French, Thomas, *York Minster: The Great East Window*, Oxford, 2003 edition
Marks, Richard, *Stained Glass in England during the Middle Ages*, London, 1993
Monckton, Linda and R. Morris (eds.), *Coventry: Medieval Art, Architecture and Archaeology in the City and its Vicinity*, The British Archaeological Association Conference Transactions XXXIII, Leeds 2011, especially Scott, Heather Gilderdale, 'John Thornton of Coventry: a Reassessment of the Role of a Late Medieval Glazier', pp. 223–39
Newton, Peter, 'Schools of Glass Painting in the Midlands, 1275–1430', unpublished PhD dissertation, University of London, 1961
Rackham, Bernard, 'The Glass-Paintings of Coventry and its Neighbourhood', *The Walpole Society* 19, 1930–1, pp. 89–110
_____ 'Faces in the Glass: A Study of the Heads', *Coventry Cathedral Chronicle* 4, 1940
Scott, Heather Gilderdale, 'The Painted Glass of Great Malvern Priory (Worcs.) c.1430–1500', unpublished PhD thesis, University of London, 2008
Sharp, Thomas, *Illustrations of the History and Antiquities of the City of Coventry*, Birmingham, 1871
Stevens, W.B. (ed.), *Victoria County History: A History of the County of Warwick*, 8, London, 1969

Index

Note: page references in **bold** refer to illustrations.

All Saints, chapel of 34–35, 39
altarpieces 57, 61, **62**, 67, **67**
Andrews, William 71
Appeal Centre 90
apse 35–36, **36**, 80, 85, 91
  illustrations **37**, **48–49**, **61**, **72**, **80**
  windows **38**, 61, **67**, **68**, 72, 81
Astley, John, plan of St Michael's **71**
Atkinson, Canon 79
Axa Equity & Law 101

Bardsley, Bishop 88
Barton Turf, Norfolk, rood screen **106**
Bayley Lane 17, 21, 35, 50
  illustrations **8–9**, **20**, **35**, **52**, **61**
Bedingfeld of Barston, Lady 61–62
bells 39, 62, 63, 68, 72, 77, 80, 93
Berkeley family 50, 54
  coffins 79
  tombs **55**
Blacking, W. H. Randall 80
Blitz Museum 93
Bohun (Bowne), George 57
Bohun family 64
  coffins 78
Botoner, Adam and William 32, 106
Branson, Richard 93
Bridgeman, Robert 80
Bridgeman family 57, 64, 70–71
  coffins 78
  monument to to Dame Mary Bridgeman **71**
Bruges tapestry 10
Buller, James 72
Burgh, John 125

campanile, proposed 68, **76**, 77
Cappers' Chamber 55, 57, 88
Cappers' Chapel 45, **52**, 53, 55
castle chapel 16, 17, 20, 24–25
cemetery 17–18, 21, 27, 28–29
chancel **25**, 35, 36, 39, **39**, **48–49**, 66
  restoration 71–72
Chapel of Industry 101
chapel of the Blessed Virgin Mary on the hill in the cemetery 21, 28–29, 34, 43, 51
Chapel of the Cross 91
Chapel of the Holy Cross 21
Chapel of the Resurrection 84
Chapel of Unity 84, 90
charnel houses *see* east crypt; west crypt
Chatwin, Philip, development of St Michael's 24, **24**
Chester, earls of 17, 20–21
Christ before Pilate, Ecce Homo (Jacob Epstein) **92**, 93
Coventry castle 17, 20, 21
Coventry Cathedral, new **18–19**, 88–93
  link to the old cathedral **44**, **85**
Crosse, John 109
Crosse's Chantry 45, 53
crypts *see* east crypt; west crypt

De Vasconcello, Josefina, *Reconciliation* 93, **94–95**
Deacon, J.R. 85, 88
Doddiscombleigh, Devon, glass **106**
Drapers' Company 27, 34, 51, 53, 54, 55
Drapers'/Lady Chapel 29, 43, 45, 50, 54, 66, 103
  post-destruction **46**, **58–59**, 82, 83, 88
Dugdale, William 109
Dyers' Chapel 45, 53, **53**, **54**, 57, 70
  monument to Dame Mary Bridgeman **71**

east crypt 34, **34**, 43, 57, 66, 79–80, 93
  door to **28**
  survival 27, **55**, 82
  Wyley Chapel 83
east end *see* apse
Edward III 7, 10
Edward the Black Prince 7
Edward VI 99
Elizabeth I, Queen 51, 55
Elizabeth II, Queen 88
Elizabeth of York, Queen 10
Epstein, Jacob, *Christ before Pilate, Ecce Homo* **92**, 93
Everitt, A.E., north porch **47**

Fairford parish church 103
Forbes, Alexander, elevation of St Michael's **56**
Forbes, Jack 83, 84
Frith, Mr 70
Fulwood, George 57

Gee, David, interior of St Michael's **25**
Gillett and Johnston 80
Girdlers' Chamber 57
Girdlers' Chapel 29, 43, 53, 55, 57, 64, 83, 84
glass
  medieval
    angel bearing a shield of the arma Christi **102**
    detail of an angel **124**, **125**
    fragment from an image of St Christopher **116**
    fragment inscribed with numbers and letters 112, **112**
    fragment showing hands laid on the head of a layman **112**
    fragments of scene of St Catherine imprisoned **117**
    group of female 'donor' figures **107**
    head (fragment) **119**
    head of a virgin saint **115**
    head of St Peter **121**
    head probably from a representation of one of the angelic Orders (fragment) **104**
    heads of a pair of laymen **111**
    Judas kissing Christ **114**
    kneeling male 'donor' figure **107**
    one of a number of groups of Apostles' heads **114**
    one of a series of monograms of the Virgin **115**
    panels showing angelic figures standing on wheels 101, **101**
    partial figure, probably from 'donor' imagery **107**
    partial figures in architectural contexts **120**
    partial head of a cleric **120**
    partial head of a male saint, probably crowned **122**
    partial head, possibly belonging to an image of one of the Nine Orders of Angels (fragment) **104**
    partial head, possibly from an image of St John **123**
    partial head, with a fillet decorated with 'oyster shell' jewels and pearl encircled jewel motif **124**
    partial inscription, reading 'Gaud(e) V(ir)go Mater' 115, **115**
    partially gabled chrismatory, held open to reveal vials of holy oil **111**
    remains of a devil in the pan of a balance, from an image of St. Michael (fragments) **103**
    remains of St James the Great, from an Apostle's Creed 110, **110**
    Resurrection 101, 113, **113**
  Victorian 81, **81**, **108**
Glazier, Thomas, of Oxford 124–25
Gloucester Cathedral 36
Godiva (Godifu), Countess 16–17
Great Malvern Priory 103, 106, 112, 115–16
Griffith, Moses, view of St Michael's from the north-west **63**
Guildhall of St Mary 7, **8–9**, **10**, **11**, 30, 109, 123

Haddon, William 50
Haigh, Mervyn G. 84
Haigh Chapel 101, 107, 113
Haye's Chantry 30
Henry II 20
Henry VI 7, 10, 99, 113
Henry VII 10
Henry Willis and Son 75
Hereford Cathedral, glass **106**
Hiorne or Hiorns, William 57, 61
  altarpiece **62**
Hollar, Wenceslaus, engravings 54, **55**, **109**
Holy Trinity 16, 17, **17**, 21, 27
Holy Well Glass 101
Howard, R.T. (provost) 81, 82, 83, 84, 101

Inge family 64
  coffins 78
International Centre 90, 93
Isabella, Queen 30

Jeayes, Henry, interior of St Michael's 63–64, **64**

Kenilworth Castle 36
King & Son 101

Lady/Drapers' Chapel 29, 43, 45, 50, 54, 55, 66, 103
  post-destruction **46**, **58–59**, 82, 83, 88
Lawrence, Prior 20
Le Vineter, John 28–29
Leland, John 51
Leofric, count of Mercia 16–17
Limesey, Robert 16
Lyons, Sir William and Lady 93

Margaret of Anjou 7, 10
Marriott, James 71
Mary, Queen 51
Matilda, Empress 17, 20
Mercers' Chapel 55, 57, 61, **61**, 79, 82
Mercers' Company 45, 51–52, 55
Merington's Chantry 30
Merton College, glass 125, **125**
Montalt, Roger and Cecily de 23
Murray, James 67
altarpiece **67**

nave 35, 39, 55, 57, 65
illustrations **25**, **39**, **40–41**, **48–49**, **60**, **64**, **67**
restoration 71–72
Nethermill, Julius 50
New College, Oxford 124, **125**
Newton, Peter 124
north aisles 27, 28, 39, 43, 45–46, **47**
box pews and galleries **64**
chapels 51, 53, 57
restoration 75
windows **68**, 69, **69**
north porch 46, **47**, **50**, 91

Owen, John 79

Paley and Austin 77
parish church, of St Michael's 20–23
Pecham, Archbishop 110
Pitcher, Sidney 101, 110
window photograph **110**
plans, of St Michael's **24**, **27**, **36**, 63, **63**, **65**, **66**, **71**
location of crypts and burial vaults **28**
orientation plan at its full extent after rebuilding **46**
vestry **77**
west crypt **78**
Poole, Benjamin 65, 66
Potter, Joseph 63
Potts and Sons 77
Preston's Chantry 45
Processional Way 35, 45
Purefoy, Dorothy 57

Queen's Way 88, **89**

Ralph (chaplain) 21
Ranulf II of Chester, Earl 20–21
Ranulf III 21
Reader, William 64–65
Reconciliation (Josefina De Vasconcello) 93, **94–95**
Rouse, Edward Clive 88
Rudge, Edward, exterior view of St Michael **62**
ruins, of St Michael's **82**, **84**, **98**
service in the ruins **83**

Scott, George Gilbert 67–68, 69
Scott, Giles Gilbert 84
Scott, John Oldrid 72, 73, 77, 100–101
drawing of the proposed campanile **76**
drawings for the restoration of the spire **73**
plan for the extension to the vestry **77**
Scott and Moffat 65
plan for the reordering of the interior **66**
Scrope, Richard 123, 125
Sharp, Thomas 64, 109
Shepey's Chantry 30, 53
Skirlaw, Walter 123
Smith, Mr (architect) 57
Smiths' (or St Andrew's) Chapel 46, 53, 55
south aisle 25–27, 35, **35**, 43, 45, **45**, 53, 68, **90**
box pews and galleries **64**
windows 88
south porch **26**, 64, 84
Spence, Basil 85, 88, 91, 101
spire 30, 39, 57, 62, 64, 70, 72–75
illustrations **14**, **42**, **72**, **73**, **75**
St Andrew's (or Smiths') Chapel 46, 53, 55
St John, chapel of 43
St Laurence's Chapel 54
St Mary, cathedral and priory 16, 17, 21, 85
St Mary, chapel of *see* chapel of the Blessed Virgin Mary on the hill in the cemetery
St Mary, parish church, North Leigh 113
St Mary's Guildhall 7, **8–9**, **10**, **11**, 30, 109, 123
St Mary's, Warwick 36
St Michael's, chapel of 16, 17, 20, 24–25
St Michael's Hall 101
St Thomas, chapel of 53
Stephen, King 17, 20
Strode family 57, 61, 64
coffins 78
Swarbrick, Thomas 57
Swillington, Lady Elizabeth 50
tomb **50**

Taylor of Loughborough 77
Thompson, John 72
Thompsons 75
Thornhill, W. Yorks 103
Thornton, John 119–20, 122–24, 125
Ticehurst, East Sussex 103
tombs 47, 50
Elizabeth Berkeley and her son Thomas (Wenceslaus Hollar engraving) 54, **55**
Lady Elizabeth Swillington 50, **50**
tower 30–32, 39, 62–63, 64, 67–68, 69–70, 72–75
illustrations **22**, **31**, **32**, **40–41**, **54**, **90**
detail **33**, **74**
east arch **73**
in scaffolding **75**
Trinity Guild 30, 43, 51, 109
Troughton, Nathaniel
interior of St Michael's **67**
north vestry door and north window in the apse **68**
westernmost window of the outer north aisle **68**

vestry 57, 61, 68, 69, 72, 74
illustrations **61**, **91**
door **68**
plans **77**
von Moellendorff, Wolf and Michael 90
Walker, J.D., north side of St Michael's and its cemetery **70**
wall paintings 43, **44**, 83, 88
Waynflete, William 99
west crypt 27, 28, **29**, **30**, 34, 43, 46, 66
air raid shelter 82
alignment 24
aumbries and piscina **43**
Chapel of the Cross 91
Chapel of Unity 84
current state 93
family vault 57, 64, 71, 78, 79
plan of **78**
Whitwell, Stedman Thomas 65
plan of St Michael's **65**
Winchester College, glass 124, **124**, 125
windows 39, 73
apse 36, **38**, 61, **67**, 72
Drapers' Chapel **58–59**
Dyers' Chapel **53**, **54**
north aisles 45, **47**, **68**, 69, **69**
restoration 57, 68–69, 73, 75
south aisle **45**, 88
tracery 72, 75, 78, **105**
see also glass
Woodcock, George 72, 75, 77
Wott, S. C., inscription **100**
Wyatt, James 63
Wyatt, John Drayton 68–69
plan of the west crypt **78**
sketch of apse and vestry extension **61**
south elevation **35**
tower, south door and Dyers' Chapel **54**
Wyken church 24
Wyley, Sir William and Lady 79–80
Wyley Chapel 83

Yeatman-Biggs, H.W., Bishop 79
effigy **46**, **79**, 88
York Minster 119, 122–24, 125